THE GOD INSANITY

Biblical Christianity Disproved

James Andre Blunt

Scriptures taken from the Holy Bible, New International Version®, NIV®. Copyright © 1973, 1978, 1984, 2011 by Biblica, Inc.™ Used by permission of Zondervan. All rights reserved worldwide. www.zondervan.com The "NIV" and "New International Version" are trademarks registered in the United States Patent and Trademark Office by Biblica, Inc.™

This book is a work of non-fiction. Unless otherwise noted, the author and the publisher make no explicit guarantees as to the accuracy of the information contained in this book and in some cases, names of people and places have been altered to protect their privacy.

Archway Publishing books may be ordered through booksellers or by contacting:

Archway Publishing
1663 Liberty Drive
Bloomington, IN 47403
www.archwaypublishing.com
1 (888) 242-5904

ISBN: 978-1-4808-7198-4 (sc)
ISBN: 978-1-4808-7199-1 (e)

Library of Congress Control Number: 2018964803

Print information available on the last page.

Archway Publishing rev. date: 12/28/2018

Contents

Preface

It is important to start this book by defining that the word "God" as used in the Title, and most places in this book does not refer to all possible concepts of God, or all possible concepts of a higher power. It is understood that some people may believe in a higher consciousness, or nature, or the universe itself as "God."

Indeed, it is not unreasonable to suggest that the universe itself is so complex and awe-inspiring that one does not need to invent a "creator." The universe, or creation itself could be "God," to some people. God could be viewed as the universal spirit that pervades or transcends everything. Therefore, most, if not all of the time, "The God Insanity," uses the word "God" narrowly, to analyze the belief in a personal, authoritarian, fear based God, such as the one clearly outlined and described in certain religious texts.

The God insanity is an illusion, or self-deception that has existed for millennia. Ancient, primitive people experienced fear and anxiety at natural phenomena, such as shooting stars, earthquakes, plagues, thunder, lightning, and even rainfall, or the lack of rainfall. In addition, they experienced fear and anxiety about multiple other things, such as diseases, and other terrible things. To explain and control these fears, they invested in defense mechanisms. A defense mechanism is an unconscious psychological mechanism that reduces anxiety arising from unacceptable, or potentially harmful stimuli.

Defense mechanisms are brought into play by the unconscious mind to manipulate, deny, or distort reality, in order to defend against feelings of anxiety, and to maintain one's self-schema. One unfortunate result of such defense mechanisms is the worldwide phenomenon seen in ancient, primitive cultures of the invention of a Supernatural being referred to as a God, or Deity. Some cultures have multiple gods, or deities, to explain such anxiety-provoking, natural, and other phenomena.

The self-schema refers to a long lasting and stable set of memories that summarize a person's beliefs, experiences, and generalizations about the self, based on any aspect of himself or herself as a person that is important to their own self definition. Once people have developed a schema about themselves, there is a strong tendency for that schema to be maintained by a bias in what they attend to, in what they remember, and in what they are prepared to accept as true about themselves. In other words, the schema becomes self-perpetuating and is then stored in long-term memory.

Early in life, we are exposed to the idea of the self from our parents, and other familiar people, including their ideas, and beliefs on religion. We begin to take on a very basic self-schema influenced by the religion of our parents. **This is why children raised in Christian homes usually grow** up to consider themselves Christians; children raised in Hindu homes usually end up considering themselves Hindu; children raised in Muslim homes usually end up considering themselves Muslim, and so on.

Most people are born as slaves, and they don't realize it even until death. They are born slaves to the religion of their parents. If they are born in a Hindu family, they think they are Hindu; if they are born in a Christian family, they usually think they are Christians, and so on with other religions, and their respective denominations.

But, very few people introspect upon why they consider themselves to be Christian, or Muslim, or Buddhist, or Hindu. Furthermore, most if not all people, believe that their religion is the right way. These days, we have people that think to themselves, that they are very liberated, or educated, because they believe all religions are true. This is also inaccurate, as they obviously haven't studied all religious doctrines thoroughly. Most religious doctrines clearly state that theirs is the only true prophet, or God, or religion.

Rarely do individuals develop enough self-esteem, as well as enough independent and critical thinking to change their self-schema based on empirical evidence and education. That is one reason, among many, as to why, even very outwardly educated people remain deeply religious in the religion that they were born into, by ignoring, denying, and rationalizing away all evidence to the contrary.

In ancient times, if people disagreed with each other's God illusion, they would probably pelt each other with stones, or fight with whatever primitive instruments they had in those days. The problem with maintaining such a God fantasy in modern times, is that nowadays, modern people in modern countries, have nuclear power at their fingertips, among other sophisticated instruments of death, that they can use if they disagree with each other's God illusion.

Obviously, it is imperative for educated, critical thinking individuals all over the world to come together, and finally put an end to all these ancient God illusions; through logic, evidence, and other scientific methods. This book is hopefully the beginning of that journey. However, this is the most difficult journey that anyone can undertake. The God illusion still has such a hold on the majority of the world, that it is entrenched, and favored in even the highest of places, from the most advanced to the most backward of countries.

Our mentality has not changed much from our cave dwelling, superstitious ancestors. We wear better clothes now, we smell better now because we have perfumes and toiletries, we have more toys to play with, more scientific knowledge, but in the end, when all is said and done, a substantial number of people today still believe in the same old unverified, superstitious stories.

In the current era, while growing up, we study history, science, and many other subjects. As a result, we probably erroneously believe that we are living in a very modern and advanced society, or culture. However, nothing could be farther from the truth. **While the world today may look outwardly advanced in comparison to the medieval ages, most of us are still very much living in an extremely primitive, backward, and superstitious culture, whether it be in the older countries of the East, or newer countries like the United States.**

Consider the following data and evidence in support of the above assertion:

(1) Even in the most advanced countries, such as the United States, most of the powerful positions, such as Supreme court justices, President of the United States, and other positions are often still filled by taking an oath on a book labeled the Holy Bible.

The only problem is that if you read through the Bible, you will find many unholy and immoral things therein. For example, there are specific stories and examples in the Bible, of the God of the Bible supporting the practice of father-daughter sex, brother-sister sex, in order to propagate the species. Detailed examples of these and other abhorrent incidents will be given in the relevant, subsequent chapters of "The God Insanity."

That is the level of backwardness, superstition, and primitiveness that we still live in today on planet Earth. Since it is impossible to explore all Gods worldwide, of all the different religions, in just one book in great depth, our main focus when referring to God in this book will be on the Biblical God as described in the Bible, though occasional reference may be made to other Gods, or other religions.

If Christianity is just a way of socio-cultural thinking, then it can be anything that society wants it to be. However, if Christianity is meant to emanate from the teachings of the Bible, then it has to be consistent with the teachings, or guidelines in the Bible. What we will discover in "The God Insanity," is that there is nothing remotely similar, or consistent, between the teachings of the Bible, versus the laws and ethics of the current United States of America, or of other modern western democracies.

Therefore, there exist two types, or levels of Christianity in the world today. The first is the socio-cultural Christianity that modern Christians in the U.S. and western culture profess to believe in. The second is the actual Biblical Christianity as specified in the Bible. There is an immense, polar opposite difference between the two. In fact, as will be shown in "The God Insanity," socio-cultural Christianity in the modern U.S. and western culture, has emerged as the victor in this battle, while Biblical Christianity has been relegated into the shadows.

Section A: The God Insanity

Introduction To Section A

People want to feel better about themselves and the world that they live in. Sometimes, that means that they need to create an illusion; whether it is a belief in an imaginary heaven, or a belief in an imaginary God. Whatever makes them feel better, even if it is a temporary feeling. Once such an illusion reaches a critical threshold, it becomes self-perpetuating across the world, and unstoppable, much like a nuclear reaction.

Sometimes, people create an illusion or a fantasy, even though it may be sub-consciously obvious to them that the fantasy is not real. There may be extreme distress if this fantasy or self-deception is challenged by logic, reason, or other scientific methods. The more the individual tries to hold onto the fantasy in the face of logic, the more distress the individual may experience.

When I was a student studying mathematics in school, I was taught that if we wanted to scientifically prove, or disprove, a theorem, we would start from a proposed hypothesis, and then proceed from there to arrive at the logical outcome or conclusions. If the conclusions were known to be factual, then we could surmise that the initial theorem was correct.

On the other hand, if we arrived at a conclusion that we knew was incorrect, then that disproved the initial theorem. Let us apply this knowledge now to prove, or disprove the existence of a God, as some humans believe in:

THE HYPOTHESIS: Firstly, let's start with the proposed hypothesis that God exists. Secondly, let us apply the following information: that this God is an all-knowing, all-powerful, and benevolent God, like so many people across the world like to believe in.

THE EVIDENCE: Now, let us look at some facts that nobody can deny. Firstly, there are terrible, terrible things that happen in the world every day. Let us try to enumerate just some of these things. These include child abuse, hunger, poverty, wars, including killing of women and children, mass shootings, accidents, illnesses and so much more. If one wanted to go on, there's volumes of books documenting some of these terrible things, such as: World War II, the holocaust, ethnic cleansings, and more.

THE CONCLUSION: So, the result is, that if we choose to believe that there exists a God, who is all-knowing, all-powerful, and benevolent; it just does not fit the evidence, as enumerated above. The reason for this is obvious: if there was an all-knowing God, he would know that there is extreme misery and evil in this world; an all-powerful, and benevolent

God would be able to use his power to rid the world of this misery and evil. Since we know for sure that there is extreme misery and evil in this world; hence, it proves beyond any doubt that there is no God, or, that if one exists, he is not all-knowing, or all-powerful, or that he is not a benevolent God.

Now, some believers will look at this evidence, and realize that their beliefs are wrong. Unfortunately, other believers will try to grasp at straws, and come up with what are called **RATIONALIZATIONS**. Chief among these rationalizations is the belief that God allows free will, and that all the bad things happening in this world are because of man's free will.

This is an absurd rationalization as shown below:

Let us examine this rationalization carefully. Now, most believers look at God as their "father," and humanity as his "children." Therefore, let us look at what society expects from parents as regards their children. If a parent were to leave the front door open, and his child runs out onto the road, and gets killed by an oncoming vehicle, the parent would be held irresponsible, and negligent. If a parent left their child unsupervised around the swimming pool, and the child fell into the pool, and drowned, the parent would be similarly considered reckless, negligent, or irresponsible.

If a parent did not provide enough food or nutrition to a child, and the child starved, the parent would be held criminally reckless, and considered negligent, and irresponsible. If a parent did not provide a safe environment for their child, and the child suffered injury, the parent would be considered negligent, irresponsible, or reckless.

A parent would not be able to argue in court that they were encouraging their child's free will. That would be laughed at. It is the parents responsibility to safeguard their children, until the children have themselves demonstrated the appropriate maturity, wisdom, and responsibility.

Similarly, a God that would let people be injured on the basis of free will, before they have proven themselves to be responsible, mature and wise in all respects: is guilty of irresponsibility, recklessness and negligence. Surely, society would not want to impose a greater level of responsibility on a human parent, as compared to the all-powerful divine parent.

Hence, if you rationalize that all of mankind's misery is the result of an all-knowing, or all-powerful God allowing free will, it leads to the inescapable conclusion that such a God is a negligent, reckless, irresponsible, and absent parent. Such a God could not be a smart, wise, or benevolent God.

Therefore, the hypothesis that an all-powerful, all-knowing, and benevolent God exists, is disproved beyond all doubt, regardless of any feeble rationalizations. Throughout the remainder of this book, more information and incontrovertible evidence will be added, to show that a Biblical God, or another personal, benevolent God just does not exist.

Chapter A1: God Is An Imaginary Projection

Most people's idea of God today, is actually an imaginary projection of what they think God should be, or what characteristics they think God should have. These mental or imaginary projections are what can be labeled as God in most people's minds.

If religious people were to actually read the Bible, or other religious books, relevant to their respective faiths, very closely; they will immediately realize that the projected Gods in their mind, may be entirely different from the God of the Bible, or the Gods in these other religious books. Since it would be an impossible task to address all the Gods of all the religions in this one book, this book devotes itself to discussing the Biblical God, and Christianity, though references may be made to other Gods, or other religions, whenever necessary. All such deviations to other Gods will be clearly identified.

Everyone potentially has the right to create whatever imaginary projection they want in their mind. However, if that projection is not consistent with the God as described in their respective religious books, then you have a twofold problem. Using Christianity and the Bible as an example, let us proceed:

The first problem is that if you believe that both your projection and the God described in the Bible is true, then you are essentially saying that there are multiple Gods. Since this goes against the one God or monotheistic theory of the Bible, either the Bible is incorrect, or your imaginary God is the false one.

The second problem is that if you choose to believe in your projected God, over the God of the Bible, then essentially you are not a religious person, per se; in that you are not a Christian, if you don't believe in the God of the Bible. The New Testament makes it very clear that a believer cannot ignore even the smallest letter from the law of the prophets in the Bible *(__Matthew 5:17-19__)*.

The above examples are just to encourage people to educate themselves, by directly reading the Bible, or other religious books themselves, and coming to their own conclusions, rather than believing in a third party's interpretation of these religious books.

For example, I was taught while growing up that Christianity and Jesus were only about love, forgiveness, and acceptance. I was extremely drawn towards these ideas from childhood to mature adulthood. Christmas brought up positive and peaceful feelings. Imagine my horror when I started reading the Bible from the beginning in the Old Testament, and found page after page of debauchery, evil, and pretty much the opposite of everything that I had been led to believe for decades. I was then told by my "Christian" friends and acquaintances to just "ignore" that pesky Old Testament part and focus on the New Testament.

I did that and discovered a twofold problem. The first is that the Old Testament is roughly almost or around 80% of the Bible. So, right off the bat, most Christians would like to ignore a substantial portion of the Bible.

The second problem is that Jesus makes it pretty clear that he is not there to destroy the law of the prophets (the Old Testament), but to fulfill it. Refer again to (***Matthew 5:17-19.***) Believing in some parts of the Bible, and rejecting other parts does not work. According to Jesus and the Bible itself, it is an "all in" or "all out" situation.

These days, some theologians, biblical scholars, and religious leaders like to pick and choose from the Bible. "I look at only the good parts," some Christians say. But, who are we to re-interpret or misinterpret clearly marked Biblical guidelines, if we truly want to be called Christians? The Bible specifies very clearly that every letter in the Bible needs to be followed:

Jesus is attributed as saying in ***Matthew 5:17-19:***

"Do not think that I have come to abolish the law or the Prophets. I have not come to abolish them but to fulfill them. For truly I tell you, until heaven and earth disappear, not the smallest letter, not the least stroke of a pen, will by any means disappear from the law until everything is accomplished. Therefore anyone who

sets aside one of the least of these Commands and teaches others accordingly will be called least in the kingdom of heaven.

All these issues will be discussed in much greater detail, and at great length, in the relevant and appropriate chapters, and sections in this book; complete with the Biblical references, and verses, for the required evidence. What "The God Insanity" will show is that the actual God described in the Bible is very different, and sometimes diametrically opposite, to the benevolent, imaginary God, of people's fantasies, inventions, and imaginary projections.

The point is that we need to be educated honestly about who it is that we believe we are praying to. If we identify ourselves as Christians, we owe it to ourselves to read the Bible on our own, without relying on a third party's interpretation of it, and see for ourselves whether our imaginary God has the same characteristics as the Biblical God.

The list of controversial passages in the Bible is extremely long, and varied, and includes passages such as ***Isaiah 13:16***:

"Their infants will be dashed to pieces before their eyes; their houses will be looted, and their wives violated."

Maybe the believers who go to church every Sunday, should inquire of their pastors, the context in which it is OK to kill babies, rape women, and put adulterers, homosexuals and non-believers to death. Specifically, such topics, and many other verses, will be dealt with in the next section of this book.

I believe that the number of atheists, or agnostics, is substantially larger in modern Western culture, than is widely reported. Most people probably go to church as a form of socializing, or as a form of automatic learned behavior, rather than from an educated belief in the God of the Bible, which can only be attained after a thorough reading of the Bible.

The majority of people in modern Western culture are probably **atheists** (don't believe in a God), or **deists** (they believe in a deity, but that deity would not be consistent with the Biblical God), or **agnostics** (unsure if a God exists), but they probably just don't know it yet.

All across our western culture, in all forms of media, whether movies, or television, or magazines, the positions and beliefs attributed to people are prima facie evidence of atheism or agnosticism. If you were to turn on late-night television to any channel, you would be presented with a bombardment of views, observations, and jokes which are mostly against the concepts clearly outlined in the Bible.

The evidence then is 100% clear. Either all these network hosts, and most of their audience members do not believe in the Bible, or they are not familiar with the laws and verses clearly outlined in the Bible. We will go into specific details on various topics in the next section of this book, **Section B: Biblical Christianity v/s modern U.S. and Western Culture**.

"The God Insanity" attempts to bring such inconsistencies into focus, and also bring into focus what the majority of people in Western culture probably already may know, albeit at a sub-conscious level: (1) that there is no Biblical God, and that religion is a fictional myth created by primitive, uneducated humans in order to keep other primitive, uneducated humans in line, and under their control. (2) that God and religion are a struggling primitive fictional fantasy, and myth, with no place in this modern open-minded world, except as a clearly recognized case of primitive fiction.

Belief in the Biblical God is much like the fairy tale "The Emperor's new clothes," wherein the Emperor is actually not wearing any clothes, but the whole population goes along with the illusion that he is, until one child points out that the Emperor has no clothes. Similarly, belief in God, much like the imaginary clothes, is an illusion that most people go along with until someone can step forward and state the obvious in a coherent, systematic and logical manner: that there is no Biblical God, just like there were no clothes on the Emperor.

The validity of the Bible in today's Western culture is also just like the "Emperor's new clothes," in the Hans Christian Andersen tale. It just doesn't exist as will be shown repeatedly in this book. The catch in the Andersen tale is that the weavers make up a story that the Emperor's clothes are not visible to those who are unfit, incompetent, or otherwise too stupid for their positions.

In the Bible, the catch is, that if you don't believe in the Bible, you'll go to hell. Both the Emperor's clothes and the Bible are stories concocted to deceive, to get the

reader to bow to the will of the people weaving the story. They are both fairy tales. We will see in **CHAPTER A2: EVIDENCE AGAINST A BIBLICAL GOD** just how deep down the rabbit hole the fairy tale of the Bible goes.

Chapter A2: Evidence Against A Biblical God

The evidence against the existence of a Biblical God is so overwhelming, as we will see here, and in other sections of this book, that to continue to believe in a Biblical God would or should qualify as a delusion. Let us examine some of this evidence:

PART 1:

If there was an all-knowing God, or an all-powerful God, and the Bible was indeed his word, we would expect volumes and volumes of useful information in the Bible, including but not limited to scientific information therein on various subjects, including physics, chemistry, biology, mathematics, astronomy, medicine, and even some kind of legal jurisprudence. If such a complex universe indeed had a creator, and the Bible is the word of that creator, we would expect the information in the Bible to sparkle with genius.

For, if indeed, an all-powerful God created this complex planet, this universe, all the variety of animal and plant life, then the word of such a creator would be full of useful information about limitless things, such as the genome,

DNA, various atoms, molecules, elements, compounds, and other such information. Surely, that would be a better way to win the respect and awe of his creations, namely us humans, rather than to maniacally pontificate about killing people, and sending them to heaven or hell.

The fact that the Bible was written by uneducated, primitive tribal people is evidenced by the fact that we see none of the above information in the Bible. No mention of atoms (like hydrogen, or oxygen), or molecules in the Bible. No mention of basic chemical reactions such as that which form water from two parts hydrogen and one part oxygen. No mention that there are billions of other planets and stars. No concept that stars are actually suns; giant balls of fire that cannot just "fall" to earth as incorrectly observed in _Revelation 9:1._

As regards _Revelation 9:1_: This is obviously not the word of some all-knowing, all-powerful God. The people writing these verses don't even appear to know or have a basic concept of what stars are. Stars cannot fall to Earth. If a star were to "fall" to Earth, it would scorch the Earth, and pull the Earth into its gravity, and consume it completely; in addition to destroying the entire solar system.

The Bible was written by and for the people living in the Bronze age, and it is an unfortunate fact that it persists even today, in having a vast influence over a modern society that can now go to the moon, and unleash nuclear war on the planet. The reasons why people today would still believe in such a fantasy is an interesting phenomenon that this book will explore in Chapter A4: "Motivations for inventing God."

Indeed, the Bible fails miserably in providing any useful, or intelligible, factual information on any topic under the Sun. In fact, it was left to numerous human scientists in different fields over the last few decades, and centuries, to discover all the vast knowledge that modern civilization has to offer. Advances in physics, chemistry, biology, mathematics, astronomy, medicine, and other subjects have come about not through study of religious works, but through human scientific endeavor, despite all manner of opposition and suppression from the church.

<u>In fact, religion has been on the wrong side of facts and history so often that it is impossible to ignore. Many of the things we now know to be true were suppressed and opposed by religion as heresy in the past.</u> One such unfortunate episode was the 1633 trial and judgment for heresy of the Italian astronomer, mathematician, physicist, and philosopher Galileo Galilei who lived from February 15, 1564 to January 8, 1642.

Biblical references in **_1 Chronicles 16:30_** and **_Psalms 93:1, 96:10, 104:5_** all essentially stated that the world is firmly established, and it cannot be moved.

Therefore, in the Christian world in the year 1616, the majority of educated people subscribed to this **geocentric** notion that the Earth was the center of the universe, and all heavenly bodies revolved around the Earth; based on the relevant Biblical verses above. **Obviously, we now know that this is completely and verifiably false. Ergo, the Bible is not the word of an all-knowing God, but of babbling primitive tribesmen.**

Flashing back to the past, many people had already proposed the correct **heliocentric** model in which the Earth and planets revolved around the Sun. One of the first persons to do so was **Aristarchus** of Samos, a Greek astronomer and mathematician who lived c. 310 - c. 230 BC. Even then, the so-called word of the Biblical God continued to propagate the false geocentric version of the Solar System for at least another 1900 years!

Nor was **Aristarchus** the only one to have figured this out. Many others including **Nicolaus Copernicus** (who lived from February 19, 1473 to May 24, 1543), **Johannes Kepler** (who lived from December 27, 1571 to November 15, 1630), and **Galileo Galilei** continued to refine the heliocentric model. Yet, even in 1616 and thereafter, the Church continued to oppose and suppress these ideas as heresy and continued to harass Galileo. By 1615, Galileo's writings had been submitted to the Roman Inquisition, and in February 1616, an inquisitorial commission declared the heliocentric model to be foolish, absurd, and heretical for explicitly contradicting the scripture!

Pope Paul V instructed **Cardinal Bellarmine** to order **Galileo** to abandon completely the opinion that the Earth moves around the Sun. For the next decade, Galileo stayed away from controversy. However, in February 1633, he was brought before an Inquisitor to be charged for speaking out again. On June 22, 1633 the sentence of the Inquisition was delivered: he was found suspect of heresy for having the opinion that the Earth is not at the center of the universe; he was sentenced to house arrest for the rest of his life and publication of any of his works was forbidden.

It is an insult to Galileo and other reasonable, logical people that a book such as the Bible filled with such fiction, fantasy, horror, and falsehoods continues to have a hold on potentially more than 2 billion people in the modern world.

PART 2:

Other important evidence for the non-existence of a Biblical God is in the verses that deal with what will happen to nonbelievers who don't believe in the God of the Bible; and instead believe in other Gods, or do idol worship. Luckily, such groups of people do exist in the modern world, so we can look at whether what is predicted in the Bible happens to them or not.

For example, (**see Chapter B9: Tolerating other religions** for further explanatory details), there are over 1 billion people in India, the majority of whom are proponents of Hinduism, which is a polytheistic religion, in that it has multiple Gods, and includes idol worship. The Bible states unequivocally that praying to other Gods, and idol worship will be punished by death. However, this group of people has flourished for more than 3000 years (look up The Indus Valley Civilization), since before the birth of Christ, and they are still in existence to this very day. We can easily see that what is predicted in the Bible does not happen to them. In other words, the God of the Bible has not struck them dead. **Ergo, the God of the Bible is a fictional character.**

Similarly, to pick another example, (**see Chapter B1: Homosexuality, and Chapter B2: Adultery** for further explanatory details), there are many adulterers, and homosexuals, or gay people alive today. The Bible states unequivocally that homosexuals will be punished by death immediately, without fail; and that adultery is punishable by death. Obviously, homosexuals and adulterers have been around for centuries, and are not dropping dead out of nowhere. In fact, we have a distinguished list of people who were adulterers, and still managed to not only become Presidents of the United States, but also managed to convince the majority of the populace that they are devout Christians, while simultaneously violating and disobeying Biblical Guidelines. **Ergo, the God of the Bible is indeed a fictional character**.

PART 3:

We know that there are billions of galaxies in the universe, each consisting of billions of stars. If there was an omnipotent God, it would reasonably follow that such a God could exert his or her influence over all these galaxies and stars. Therefore, exerting his influence all over a tiny little planet called Earth would be fairly easy. If so, why is it that the influence of this omnipotent Biblical

God was present only in a tiny, backward geographical area of the Middle East?

How come that 2000 to 3000 years ago, this omnipotent God was not able to exert any influence in India, China, northern Europe, and other such parts of the world? The answer is fairly simple, and obvious. It is not some imaginary, omnipotent God that wrote the Bible, but humans with limited knowledge, and limited geographical influence.

Let us explore this further and consider the example of Jesus himself. Many questions come to mind. If Jesus indeed did have divine power, why were his appearances so extremely limited in terms of both time and geography? Let us clarify that question further. As far as the issue of time is concerned, nobody in the whole wide world has been proven to have seen or heard from Jesus in approximately 2000 years.

Furthermore, as to the issue of geography, nobody in the whole world, outside of the limited Middle Eastern areas described in the Bible, has ever personally seen him, or heard from him, even during the time that he is supposed to have lived. He was never seen in, or heard from, in China, India, Europe, Australia, or hundreds of other places even during his supposed lifetime.

There is nothing divine, or extraordinary about that. The average human being alive today has travelled over a wider area, and to more countries than is ever attributed to Jesus in the Bible. This shows that the authors of the Bible were limited in their knowledge of geography, and could not have been writing the word of an imaginary, all-powerful God. Nor is it possible that the influence of such an all-powerful God, or his supposed divine son Jesus, would be so limited in area, to just a backward part of the Middle East, and surrounding areas.

This is absolute proof of the lack of any divine power in the story of this otherwise extraordinarily remarkable young man. If an individual was actually imbibed with divine power, we would have proof of appearances by him, more widespread in terms of both geography and time. What that means is that people would've seen or heard from him in person all over the world, and not just in a limited area of the Middle East, and surrounding areas. Secondly, he would not have just disappeared for 2000 years.

In those terms, he is no different than any other ordinary human being that ever lived, nor does he have any other unusual powers. As far as the issue of the supposed miracles that are attributable to Jesus in the Bible, these will be examined in more detail in **Chapter A8: The Superstitions of Jesus**. For now, let us examine all the different geographical areas around the world, to see what, if any, evidence, there was for the existence of, or presence of Jesus in those regions:

Russia and **China**: No evidence for the existence of, or presence of Jesus, in this area during his supposed lifetime.

India: No evidence for the existence of, or presence of Jesus, in this area during his supposed lifetime. This region has its own set of myths and stories of beings with divine power, none of whom resemble Jesus even remotely. These are the Lords Shiva, Rama, Vishnu, Krishna, Brahma, as well as a pantheon of other Gods / Goddesses with nothing in common with Biblical stories.

Northern Europe: No evidence for the existence of, or presence of Jesus, in this area during his supposed lifetime. This area also had its own pantheon of Gods: Thor, Odin, and others with no resemblance to Biblical scripture.

Southern Europe: This includes the Greek Gods, and Goddesses, such as Apollo, Ares, Aphrodite, Artemis, and so many more. No evidence for the existence of, or presence of Jesus, in this area during his supposed lifetime.

North American Native Americans: The spiritual practices of the indigenous people of the Americas included a combination of monotheistic, polytheistic, henotheistic theology with no mention or similarity to Biblical scripture, or Jesus.

We can now see that the same pattern repeats itself wherever we go. Other than a tiny part of a backward area of the Middle East, and surrounding Egypt, there is no evidence for a Biblical God, or Jesus 2000 years ago. How is that possible? The supposed creator of the whole universe, all the billions and billions of galaxies, each with billions of stars, and of the tiny planet Earth; and

the influence of this genius creator does not even extend to the whole of the planet Earth as it stood 2000 years ago, but to just a remote Middle Eastern area, and surrounding Egypt. Furthermore, the word of this supposed God in the Bible basically constituted in giving guidelines that are already obsolete in the modern era (see Chapters B1 - B10). It takes a truly greatly delusional mind to still believe in the existence of a Biblical God.

As we see above, there have been a pantheon of Gods, and Goddesses, all over the world; and none of those myths, or stories, match up with each other. Most civilizations created their own independent myths. Furthermore, none of these stories are really special compared to one another, because they all follow the same format: which is the attribution of divine powers to individuals, some of whom are pure fiction, and never existed; and some who may have actually lived and died as regular human beings. It is amazing how much influence these pieces of ancient fiction, or fantasy, still have in the world today. Unfortunately, that shows us just how very primitive, and backward the world is even today, despite all our modern scientific, and other advances.

Furthermore, people who pedal such fiction and fantasy continue to have immense power in the world today. As I write this chapter, a famous evangelical preacher just died at the age of 99 years old. I was amazed in reading about his life as to how much power he held in terms of his contacts with numerous United States presidents, and other famous or powerful people, in addition to millions of other followers.

Interestingly, the world we live in is still so backward, that all this influence and power is as a direct result of secondhand peddling of pure fantasy and fiction. That just tells us of the extremely backward state that the world is in, even in the beginning of the 21st century. We will explore what causes modern humans to continue to believe in such centuries old fictional fantasies in **Chapter A4: Motivations for Inventing God**. But first, let's examine if there could be a God in the next **Chapter A3: What if there was a God?**

Chapter A3: What If There Was A God?

Could there be sentient beings more powerful than us, who could do things that we (humans) can't imagine? Of course, that's possible. Even humans today can do things that humans couldn't imagine 40 years ago, or a 100 years ago, or a 1000 years ago.

But that doesn't mean that we are Gods. In fact, even to humans who lived 2000 years ago, it might seem that we are Gods, because of our advanced technology. We have machines that can make us fly! We can circle the Earth! We have machines that can hover in the air, and unleash terror from the sky, in the form of automatic gunfire, rockets, and missiles. We have machines that can fire nuclear weapons from afar. Can you imagine how a goat herder living 2000 years ago would interpret that? But, in that sense, Gods are just advanced beings that have more technology, and can do more things than us.

Let us consider and explore the following scenario: imagine what would happen if representatives of the modern human race alive today, could go back in time 2000 years ago, along with a wide variety of representative samples of modern civilian, and military technology. Alternatively, let us consider what would happen if tribal nomads from the Middle East 2000 years ago, somehow found themselves in our modern world.

The irony is, that if these ancient, primitive tribal people that lived in the time that the Bible was written, ran into modern humans, with all of our modern technology, they would undoubtedly consider us to be Gods. It is a situation of extreme dramatic irony, that modern humans instead look backwards towards these ancient outlandish texts, written in the time of primitive goat herders, as the word of God.

Let us try to imagine what these primitive tribal men, or women would think if they saw our modern technology unleashed? Let us consider just some of these technologies:

(1) Nuclear weapons that can kill billions of people; more people than the fictional Biblical God kills in the whole fictional Bible. These weapons can create an Armageddon on Earth, which will make the imaginary hell fires of these primitive peoples' nightmares, timid by comparison. The power to wipe out not just an ancient city, or continent, but the entire world many times over; blotting out the Sun, and plunging the planet into darkness, and nuclear winter, for many years.

(2) Automatic weapons, and modern protective armor that could allow one modern human to take on, and wipe out an entire army of ancient tribes men.

(3) Modern medicines that could cure leprosy, tuberculosis, plague, or other diseases dreaded by these primitives. These medicines could give the gift of life and health to these primitives beyond their wildest imaginations.

(4) Biological and chemical weapons that would make the plagues in the Bible look timid by comparison.

When you consider all of the above, it is literally fact that just a 2000 year technological advantage, can translate into one modern human armed with the right technology, having God like power over these ancient tribes people; whether it is the power to give life, or take it away on a massive scale that they could never imagine.

Nothing in the Bible narrative can compare to what modern humans can actually unleash on this planet today. Modern humans have access to more destructive power today than the fictional Biblical God created by primitives 2000 years ago. And yet, some modern humans still worship the rubbish writings of these ancient, uneducated tribes people as the word of God. If that is not delusional, then I don't know what is.

In fact, if we were to grant for the sake of this discussion, that there is a God; logic would dictate that it would be someone, who would in turn, have a 2000 year

technological advantage over even modern humans. Such an advanced alien would not be obsessed with the sexual proclivities, and other day to day activities, of a primitive race, and thus would have nothing in common with the fictional Biblical God, invented by primitive tribal people, to keep other primitive tribal people in a tiny backwater area of the planet Earth under their control.

Chapter A4: Motivations For Inventing God (Why Religions Survive)

I n this Chapter, we will look at some of the reasons why religion still survives in the modern world, and what motivates people to keep on believing in a fictional, benevolent God, despite overwhelming evidence to the contrary.

(1) Childhood indoctrination:

One of the major reasons that religion still survives in the world today, is that the majority of people are unable to come out of the indoctrination that they undergo at the hands of their parents, grandparents, family, and society while growing up. This indoctrination is passed down from one generation to another, to the next generation, so that even after hundreds of years, it still persists; despite there being so many scientific, and other advancements in knowledge in the modern world.

That is why a Roman Catholic from Goa can argue for hours and hours, using pseudo-scientific jargon about why Jesus is the one true messiah. By the same token, a Muslim from

Saudi Arabia can argue continuously as to why Mohammed is the last, true, final prophet. This kind of phenomena repeats endlessly all over the world. The actual prima facie evidence staring at everyone, the so-called "elephant in the room," escapes them all: that they are all arguing (in most, if not all cases), in favor of the religion that each of them was born into.

In the few cases where people born in one religion do switch to another religion, these cases are rare. Furthermore, no religion has a monopoly on this kind of conversion. People from any and all religions do occasionally convert to other religions depending upon many factors. A detailed discussion of this is unnecessary for the purposes of this book. Briefly, as an example, when people migrate to a country that has a different majority religion than their own, they sometimes, on rare occasions, convert to their new country's majority religion.

The lack of self-confidence, and financial as well as psychological dependency that most children have upon their parents, or elders, ensures that whatever self-schema the parents or elders impose upon the child, takes a strong hold from birth. As has been mentioned earlier, most people are born as slaves, and they don't realize it even till death. This is why children raised in Christian homes usually grow up to consider themselves Christians; children raised in Hindu homes usually end up considering themselves Hindu; children raised in Muslim homes usually end up considering themselves Muslim, and so on.

It takes strong people with well developed reasoning abilities to overcome these indoctrinations, and come out of these fantasy stories passed down for hundreds of years, through several generations. These strong people have the necessary resilience to do the necessary research, and become consciously aware of the truth. They do not trade in their need to be liked, or their dependency on their parents, and society, by submitting to these indoctrinations.

When humans are little children, they are like parrots and monkeys. They mimic whatever they see around them, and say whatever they hear around them. Thus, imaginary concepts like God, or prayer, get ingrained into them at an early age, depending upon the particular God that their parents, or extended families follow.

As they grow older, this becomes more ingrained in the form of automatic behavior. They may become very educated, some may become scientists, or Presidents, but some of them are never able to escape those early, ingrained, automatic experiences, and learned behavior.

This then results in seemingly reasonable people fighting with each other over what imaginary friend in the sky they follow, or whose imaginary friend is real. Obviously, none of these imaginary friends are real. Yet, these automatic behaviors persist well into adulthood, and into death.

Hence, we see that much of humanity these days is born into slavery, much like the science-fiction movie "The Matrix."

However, unlike some futuristic, advanced, artificial intelligence, or machine; most humans are born into slavery based on books written by ancient, uneducated, tribal nomads whose values modern society, and parents still continue to impose upon their children even today from the moment of their birth.

This is the most despicable, and widespread form of slavery present in the modern world today. Almost every child born in the world today is exposed to these ideas at an impressionable age, when the child has not yet developed any logic or reason.

Once a child is imprinted with these ideas, in all likelihood, the child becomes a slave to these ideas, for the rest of his, or her life. Some people are able to break this bond of slavery enough to research what their holy books actually say, and ask the pertinent, and relevant questions.

<u>This modern day psychological slavery is one of the most critical and pressing issues of our time.</u> This book attempts to shed light on these processes, with the hope that one day, humanity will finally be able to break these modern chains of slavery that go back hundreds, or thousands of years.

<u>The wish for a creator is the unrealistic fantasy, or fairy tale wish of a child, who is unable, or unwilling to grow up.</u> It is the wish for an idealized parent that will never go away. In that sense, the majority of adults alive in the

world today, are still children, who believe in a fantasy fairy tale that will never come true.

(2) Automatic learned behavior:

Once the belief in a God, or religion has been indoctrinated in a child, this belief persists due to the phenomenon of automatically learned behavior that happens in humans at a subconscious level. Humans see other people use the word "God" in a certain context, internalize it, and then begin using it themselves in similar contexts.

This happens automatically, and subconsciously, without any logical thought or purpose. Examples are mass shootings, or different disasters, such as: hurricanes, tornadoes, or other forms of mass casualty.

The word "God" describing an invisible, all-powerful entity that no one has ever seen, or heard from, is invoked each time. A better word indeed would be a word like "fate" or "destiny," if one believed in such a thing.

Those words more accurately describe the human experience. For, if humans are born, they must die. That is an absolute truth. It has never been disproved, ever in our history. So that is our fate, or destiny, and more accurately describes the process.

I will go off tangent for a moment here to address those people that might be thinking, "but Jesus was resurrected." Without getting into an argument on the merits of that claim, the fact remains that he did "die" in order to get resurrected. Furthermore, he has not been heard from, or been seen, since then.

Most scholars are of the opinion that even the disciples of Jesus believed that he would return in their lifetime. See **_Matthew 24:34_** below. Only when he did not, and successive generations noticed that he did not return as promised, that they then began the task of preparing and documenting the New Testament.

Matthew 24:34

"Truly I tell you, this generation will certainly not pass away until all these things have happened."

So, we get back to my point, that it is an absolute fact that all humans must die at some point. The only unknown issue is how they are going to die. If you live in a region that has hurricanes, you might die from a hurricane. But you can also die from hundreds of other different reasons, or causes. There is no invisible, all-powerful entity called "God" involved in birth, or death. Plants, animals, and any or all other living organisms die just like humans. There is nothing really special about it. It is just what it is.

(3) Parental control:

If you think about it carefully, the invention of God is just another level of control. As children grow older, they

start to see that their parents are humans with all kinds of human weaknesses, and emotions.

What better way to continue to control children as they grow up into adults than to invent a larger than life parent; in other words, a God. Larger organizations such as theocratic governments also use this larger than life parent (God) to control vast segments of their population as well.

Fortunately, in the process of inventing a God or Gods, primitive people left behind volumes of pages of data, in the form of various so-called holy books. As a result, when a reasonable, modern day reader with critical thinking skills reads these books, for example, the Bible; it is glaringly obvious to them that the God of the Bible has all the qualities of a petty, jealous, over-controlling parent. This proves that religion is just an extension of parental control.

<u>(4) Threats of torture and execution</u>:

Even in the current era, an examination of religion is still punishable by torture, death, and execution in some theocratic, religious countries. How are people supposed to examine religion in a reasonable fashion with the threat of death, torture, and societal ridicule hanging over their heads? Such is the backward state of affairs even in the 21st century in some countries. A big motivation for continuing to believe in religion, or pretending to do so, has been the fear of being persecuted in this manner.

It was not that far back when even the modern, advanced, western democracies used to torture and kill their people for examining religion with a scientific eye. In most modern western countries, this does not happen today. However, discrimination against a critical examination of religion is still present even in some modern western countries to this day.

An adult, logical conversation on religion is long overdue. In modern Western society, we have only just begun to be able to discuss religion in a logical and rational manner. Even so, religion has a vast control over mankind and it's most powerful institutions, including governments. The United States was at the forefront of separating church and state at the time of the founding of this country. As such, the United States was far ahead of its time in this regard.

(5) Fear of chaos, bad luck, injury, disease, disability, death and the unknown:

Life is full of unpredictability, chaos, and bad luck. Clearly, people fear this unpredictability, chaos, and bad luck; and they experience conscious and subconscious discomfort because of this. This is very natural.

The list of things to fear is virtually limitless: whether it is a plane crash, or accident, cancer, poverty, disease, injury, or other unknowns. This is similar to the primitive, superstitious, and delusional belief in ancient times of warding off evil spirits. In fact, even in modern times, in some countries in the world, life still revolves around the notion of warding off evil spirits.

The invention of God tries to create an illusion of control over such things. Manifestly, some people believe that by giving respect and deference to this higher power, or God, they can control some of this unpredictability, chaos, and bad luck. Due to this, otherwise seemingly rational people tend to shut out all logic and reasoning. They end up blindly believing in whatever faith they were raised in as a means to control this fear and discomfort.

It is understandable. Life can sometimes be cruel, unpredictable, and chaotic. It may be tempting to create an imaginary entity called God, who potentially has control over all the bad things that could potentially happen to you. But creating a delusion to deal with your fears is not the correct solution, especially now in the 21st-century. The situation that a drastic number of people in the world even today believe in such a delusion is a pathetic reminder of how backward humanity still is.

Another motivation that primitive, uneducated, tribes men had to invent religion, and Gods, was to try and explain fearful phenomena, such as thunder, lightning, rain, and other things that would have been very scary in the Bronze age. Thus, we see that the northern Europeans had **Thor**, the God of thunder, lightning and rain; ancient Hindus had **Indra**, the God of thunder, lightning and rain, and so on.

All over the world, there existed the invention of deities and Gods by primitives to try and explain natural, and other phenomena. However, in the modern world, we don't need God to explain these phenomena, whether it be a Thor, or Indra, or the Biblical God.

Most of humanity is still a slave to a delusion or fantasy created thousands of years ago, when illiterate people did not have any scientific basis to explain many of the natural phenomena, and were compelled to create an imaginary, all-powerful entity to pray to. That this persists in the 21st-century is an amazing reminder of how billions of people still don't have independent reason and thought, despite claims to the contrary.

(6) The illusion of comfort:

The God fantasy and religion can give some people a sense of comfort. They feel that if a higher power protects them, then they will be safer from all the bad things that could potentially happen to them, such as: accidents, disability, disease, death, or other scary things. This is completely natural. Sometimes, this illusion of comfort can be a very powerful tonic and just what one needs.

It is similar to a placebo in modern medicine. A placebo is an inert substance, or chemical, usually without any harmful, or good properties, that is given to people who are under the impression that they are getting a medicine. Incredibly, placebos can sometimes work as well or better than a new medicine being tested in clinical trials. This is because the mind can be a powerful weapon. It can accelerate healing, or the feeling of getting better if it thinks that it is getting a medicine.

Similarly, even though belief in a God, or a religion may be illusory, if the mind believes it, it can certainly make people feel better sometimes. However, it is still a placebo. It should not become something that the majority of the world lives by every day, just because it can sometimes provide comfort. We have to find a more real solution for comfort; just like doctors these days don't depend upon placebos to treat their patients.

(7) Fear of social isolation or ridicule:

By the time people have grown up enough to have a brain that can now think, analyze, research, and reason; most, if not all, of their contacts, friends, relatives, and social circle are already ingrained with the same mass religious or God fantasy that they themselves have grown up with.

Analyzing or reasoning about these matters now risks alienating the group and isolating the individual. Fear of isolation, therefore, keeps the mass fantasy intact long after grown-up adults have developed a fully developed, and functional brain.

It is only the strong, independent people, or people that cannot tolerate fools that are able to get out of this network of mass fantasy. One must be strong enough to step back from the influence of social connections to see the mass fantasy for what it is.

The more that some people get enmeshed in relationships with family, or friends, the more they may be unable to grow as critical thinking, independent individuals, unless their family members or friends are themselves mature, independent, critically thinking individuals. It is only once one is able to get away from negative enmeshed relationships, that one can truly develop as an independent, critically thinking person.

This is one of the many reasons that religions still survive to this day. Most people are dependent upon enmeshed relationships for their emotional comfort, or for financial, or employment related reasons. If the community or society around them tends to favor a particular God illusion, most people are unable to break free of that God illusion.

Sometimes, due to loneliness, fear, and insecurity, some people have the need to create a supernatural friend, aka God. In the 2000 American film, "Cast Away," Tom Hank's character called Chuck is marooned and isolated on an island. He finds a Wilson volleyball in one of the packages that came ashore with him. We see how the need to create an imaginary friend causes him to draw a face on the Volleyball and call it Wilson. He begins talking to it, and it probably helps him survive on the island.

Chuck's need for a friend in the movie is analogous to some people's need to invent God. However, most of us are not marooned on an isolated island. Therefore, in their need to invent God, these people are actually demonstrating to us that they still feel lonely, isolated, and insecure. This is, of course, natural to some extent. There is, after all, so much chaos and unpredictability in the world, as has been discussed before.

(8) Fake politeness and political correctness:

Another reason why religion continues to survive and flourish in modern society is the sad epidemic of fake politeness and political correctness that gets selectively applied, or mostly applied to religious discussions in modern culture.

In this alternate reality, any attempt to have a reasonable or logical discussion about religion is instantly viewed as an attack, or a threat. The reason that this happens is because religious backers are acutely aware of the nebulous foundations on which religion continues to exist. If there was a strong ground or foundation for the validity of religion, religious folks would not fear reasonable or logical discussion, but would in fact, welcome it.

(9) Psychological bribing:

This occurs in many religions in the form of preaching that the kingdom of God, or heaven awaits after death. The message is: believe us, and you will live happily ever after in a fictional heaven. Don't believe us, and we will come after you with torture, death, and stories of a fictional place called hell. It is basically the classical carrot and stick situation.

Of course, the part that heaven and hell are fictional places created by terrified, uneducated, primitive peasants that lived thousands of years ago is conveniently left out. However, all these ideas survive even today in some modern humans, because of successive generations of childhood indoctrination, automatic learned behavior, and parental control as shown earlier in this chapter.

However, and very importantly, as will be shown now, is that even if you believe that a heaven exists, the chances that you will enter heaven are essentially zero, according to the Bible itself. We will see in **Section B** how tough the Biblical guidelines are in terms of entering heaven. A believer has to follow every letter of the law in the Bible as has been pointed out many times in this book. Refer to **_Matthew 5:17-19_** again. Therefore, you have to give away ALL your money to the poor (see **Chapter B8**); NEVER get divorced or have an affair (see **Chapter B2**); turn the other cheek always (see **Chapter B10**) and follow numerous other guidelines.

Let me be very clear. The possibility that any person in modern western culture could have followed ALL of these guidelines is very remote. Hence, it is very farfetched that any person will be entering the kingdom of heaven, even if you believe in a heaven fantasy. Look at all the following Biblical verses for proof:

Matthew 7:21-27:

"Not everyone who says to me, 'Lord Lord,' will enter the kingdom of heaven, but only the one who does the will of my father who is in *heaven.*" ..... *"Therefore everyone who hears these words of mine and puts them into practice is like a wise man who built his house on the rock. The rain came down, the streams rose, and the winds blew and beat against that house, yet it did not fall, because it had its foundation on the rock. But everyone who hears these words of mine and does not put them into practice is like a foolish man who built his house on sand. The rain came down, the streams rose, and the winds blew and beat against that house, and it fell with a great crash."*

Essentially, what the Bible is saying is that you can take the name of the Lord as much as you like, but if you are not doing the things mentioned in the Bible, you are going to hell, and not to heaven. Even just taking a minuscule number of examples mentioned elsewhere in the Bible, and discussed in **Chapters B1-10** of this book, if you are rich and do not give away ALL of your possessions to the poor, or if you have premarital sex, or if you divorce and remarry, and numerous other things; you are going against the teachings of the Bible, and therefore, cannot go into heaven.

Some people may want to rationalize that they can always seek forgiveness, and enter the kingdom of heaven. In fact, most churches rely on this fantasy to entice people to attend. This is completely against what the Bible teaches. There is ample evidence in the Bible, that forgiveness will not be an option. Let us explore the passages in the Bible that deal with the subject of forgiveness:

Joshua 24:19

"Joshua said to the people, "You are not able to serve the LORD. He is a holy God; he is a jealous God. <u>He will not forgive your rebellion and your sins.</u>"

Proverbs 1:24-33

"<u>But since you refuse to listen when I call and no one pays attention when I stretch out my hand, since you disregard all my advice and do not accept my rebuke,</u> I in turn will laugh when disaster strikes you; ..... Then <u>they will call to me but I will not answer; they will look for me but will not find me, ... they did not accept my advice and spurned my rebuke,</u> they will eat the fruit of their ways and be filled with the fruit of their schemes .... but whoever listens to me will live in safety and be at ease, without fear of harm."

Essentially, what this means is, that if you have neglected the teachings of the Bible, in terms of, for example, if you have accumulated wealth, or been divorced, or remarried, or committed adultery, you will not be able to find forgiveness from God when God's punishment finally arrives, no matter how much you profess to believe in God, or profess to follow the path of God.

Some priests, or Biblical scholars may want to say that there is substantially more forgiveness in The New Testament. However, I refer you back to Jesus, who is attributed as saying in ***Matthew 5:17-19:***

"Do not think that I have come to abolish the law or the Prophets. I have not come to abolish them but to fulfill them. For truly I tell you, until heaven and earth disappear, not the smallest letter, not the least stroke of a pen, will by any means disappear from the law until everything is accomplished. Therefore anyone who sets aside one of the least of these Commands and teaches others accordingly will be called least in the kingdom of heaven.

Jesus himself says that anyone who tries to set aside any of the Biblical guidelines from The Old Testament, and teaches others accordingly, will be called least in the kingdom of heaven. In addition, Jesus is very clear that he himself is not here to set aside any of The Old Testament guidelines. That puts him in a very conflicted situation when he tries to do exactly that in The New Testament.

So, what is the anti-dote to the heaven fantasy, one might ask? How does one break away from the slavery of the heaven fantasy? The answer goes somewhat like this: People are generally afraid of dying because they are afraid that they have not fulfilled their purpose in life, or achieved what they wanted to achieve. In other words, they have not yet lived the full, unrestricted life of their purpose, or fantasy; or possibly are still struggling to find purpose and meaning in their current life.

Hence, believing in an alternate (albeit imaginary), fantasy place called heaven gives them a loophole in terms of feeling that they will still get another chance to fulfill their purpose. Obviously, the antidote to this is to start the journey to figure out one's purpose here and now. After that, one has to actually work hard, and do whatever one needs to do in the current life to achieve that purpose. This may be a lot more difficult than it sounds. However, giving up and believing in a heaven where one gets another chance is just fantasy and escapism.

The whole concept of heaven is based on the procrastination mentality of "I will do it tomorrow (in heaven presumably), what I should be doing today." <u>If you were really able to find your purpose in life and fulfill it, you would not be worried about going to heaven, or what happens to you after death. Heaven becomes irrelevant, and obsolete.</u>

<u>(10) Rationalization and denial:</u>

<u>Rationalization</u> is a defense mechanism in which controversial behaviors or feelings are justified, and explained in a seemingly rational or logical manner to avoid the true explanation. <u>Denial</u> is a defense mechanism in which a person is faced with a fact that is too uncomfortable to accept, and rejects it instead, insisting that it is not true despite overwhelming evidence.

These defense mechanisms play a big part in people trying to explain away obvious evidence or data that disproves religion or shows the negatives of religion. Examples of rationalizations are peppered in a few different places in this book such as the <u>rationalization of free will</u> in the Introduction to Section A; and the <u>rationalization of Incest</u> in Chapter B4.

How do you have a rational discussion with people who can rationalize everything away? It is important to identify those rationalizations and bring them out into the open for everybody to see.

(11) Ignorance:

Many people in the modern United States still believe that most of our modern ethics and guidelines emanate from the Bible. This kind of ignorance is commonplace, and even seasoned politicians have been known to make statements along the lines of, "We are a Judeo-Christian nation." This is simply not true. As will be shown in Chapters B1-10, most, if not all, of the values, ethics and laws of the modern United States are completely opposite to what is preached in the Bible.

(12) Maintaining law and order:

This reason has been given as an incentive, or motivation for the invention of God, so people will be afraid of committing crimes; thus ensuring law and order. Indeed, 2000 years ago, there were no rules of federal procedure, no state laws, or city and county ordinances, or organized law enforcement to take care of lawless acts. In those primitive times, it may have made sense to invent an all-powerful being that would strike you down for committing rape, murder, or other criminal actions.

This should sound very insulting to modern believers, as it makes it appear that without a God, or religion, these

people would be just out on the streets performing all manner of lawless acts. Now, maybe that's true. But these days, we have all manner of civil and criminal codes, or laws to ensure law, order and safety.

(13) Gives purpose:

Most people are still not ready to hear the truth, or give up their Gods. This is because some people have not yet found their own unique purpose, or individual purpose separate from their Gods. Unfortunately, purpose derived from religion alone is likely to have bad consequences resulting in the people of one religion fighting with the people of another religion.

(14) Fear of unhappiness:

To try to overcome unhappiness, people invent, or create an imaginary, all-powerful friend, or protector, such as a God. Unfortunately, some people's lives are so unhappy, that the only hope they can muster, is a belief in the afterlife, or a belief in heaven, or God, as a means of escaping from the painful reality in the here and now.

We see the evidence of unhappiness in people's lives these days by the rapid rise in rates of mental illness, depression, suicide, and substance use, such as opioid use. Many people live a secret, quiet life filled with misery and unhappiness. According to a USA TODAY article, more than 47,000 Americans killed themselves in 2017. Since 1999, the suicide rate has climbed by 33 percent. Suicide is the 10th leading cause of death in the United States.

It is, therefore, tempting to believe in a heaven, a God, or an afterlife, with the motivation to escape from their painful circumstances. Religion may give them comfort as a means to make life more tolerable, possibly preventing extreme measures like suicide or other forms of acting out.

The basic perceived benefit of religion is that people get to control their unhappiness, fear, and anxiety about unexpected and bad things happening to them by putting their faith in a higher power who they can in turn presumably influence through prayer.

However, this reprieve is likely to be temporary and harmful in the long run. Deep down, people may realize that all these stories of heaven, God, and an afterlife are nothing but fiction, making them feel even worse. Therefore, better solutions than a belief in these fictional stories are needed.

The only way to overcome these feelings of unhappiness, fear, and anxiety without resorting to a delusion, is, of course, to realize and accept that there is chaos in the world which is not under our control; that despite this chaos, we can plan for, and enjoy good things, and plan for, or prepare for any bad things.

(15) Recovering from drugs and alcohol:

Believing in a higher power is sometimes considered useful in giving people the courage and help to overcome addictions from drugs or alcohol as in AA, Alcoholics Anonymous. However, this higher power need not just be a personal God. It has been discovered that people can get sober by believing in each other, and in the strength of their group.

Chapter A5: Creationism Equals Incest, Polygamy And Sexual Slavery

To believe in creationism, according to the Bible's narrative of Genesis, is to believe that all humans currently living on Earth are products of incest, polygamy, and sexual slavery. The Bible does not leave this to the imagination. It describes many kinds of incest: father-daughter incest, brother-sister incest, and so on. It similarly describes polygamy and sexual slavery in numerous places. It is to be noted that all of this happens under the support and direction of the God of the Bible.

Furthermore, the Bible's assertion that all of humanity is a product of incest is not limited to a few passages, or a few stories. These stories are so numerous that some of them will be examined in **Chapters B4 and B5**. However, a brief overview of some of these stories is presented here:

(1) Noah:

Genesis 6:7-7:24:

According to this story, every living thing was wiped out from the Earth, including man and beast. The only humans to survive were Noah, and those who were with him in the ark. Specifically Noah, his wife, his three sons, the three wives of Noah's sons; along with one pair of all the other living creatures.

Here again, the incestuous overtones are found. Since all human life was completely wiped out, it follows all of humanity is descendant from Noah and his family in the ark. This all clearly happens under the direction of the God of the Bible, for it is he who brings the great flood, and saves Noah and his three sons, for the purpose of repopulating the earth.

It is further clarified in ***Genesis 9:18-19*** that it is indeed from these people that all the Earth's population arose:

The sons of Noah who came out of the ark were Shem, Ham and Japheth. Ham was the father of Canaan. <u>These were the three sons of Noah, and from them came the people who were scattered over the whole earth.</u>

Further clarification and proof of incest is provided in ***Genesis 10:1-5***

This is the account of Shem, Ham and Japheth, Noah's sons, who themselves had sons after the flood. The sons of Japheth: Gomer, Magog, Madai, Javan, Tubal, Meshek and Tiras.

The sons of Gomer: Ashkenaz, Riphath and Togarmah.

The sons of Javan: Elishah, Tarshish, the Kittites and the Rodanites.

From these the maritime peoples spread out into their territories by their clans within their nations, each with its own language.

As if the story of Noah is not enough, the Bible provides more proof of incest, sometimes intertwined with rape, polygamy, and sexual slavery complete with a whole cast of Biblical characters in many places. Consider the following examples from these Biblical verses:

(2) Lot and his daughters:

Genesis 19:31-38: discusses father-daughter incest, wherein Lots daughters essentially rape their father in order to produce offspring. They do this by giving him wine till he passes out, and thereafter both daughters take turns having sex with him.

(3) Abraham and Sarah (brother-sister incest):

Genesis 20:11-13: discusses brother and sister incest between Abraham and Sarah (who are technically half siblings) as follows:

Abraham replied, "I said to myself, 'There is surely no fear of God in this place, and they will kill me because of my wife.' Besides, <u>she really is my sister, the daughter of my father</u>, though not of my mother; <u>and she became my wife</u>. And when God had me wander from my father's household, I said to her, 'This is how you can show your love to me: Everywhere we go, say of me: "He is my brother."

<u>Note that all this happens under the guidance of the God of the Bible. When Abimelech tries to take Abraham's sister/wife for himself, God comes to Abraham's rescue and convinces Abimelech to return Sarah, and calls Abraham a prophet</u> in *<u>Genesis 20:7</u>*:

"Now return the man's wife, for he is a prophet, and he will pray for you and you will live. But if you do not return her, you may be sure that you and all who belong to you will die."

<u>Therefore, the God of the Bible explicitly supports the marriage and sexual relationship between Abraham and Sarah, who are actually half brother and sister.</u>

<u>(4) Jacob and Rachel:</u>

An example of incest, polygamy and sexual slavery is the Biblical story of Jacob, and his marriage to his two cousins, AND their respective slave girls. Depending upon which Biblical version and verse you read, some verses indicate that Jacob is the Brother of Laban making him the girls' uncle; other passages seem to indicate that Jacob is actually Laban's nephew, thus making him the cousin of the 2 girls he marries:

Jacob meets Rachel, his cousin in **_Genesis 29:12:_**

"He had told Rachel that he was a relative of her father and a son of Rebekah. So she ran and told her father."

Between **_Genesis 29:15-35_** Jacob ends up getting both of Laban's daughters, Leah and Rachel as his wives, and having sexual relations with both of them. Note that Laban gives his two daughters to Jacob in lieu of his wages.

Between **_Genesis 30-30:13_**, both of Jacob's wives Rachel and Leah give Jacob their respective slave girls / maidservants, Bilhah and Zilpah, to have sexual relations with and children are born from these sexual relations.

Thus, in one fell swoop, incest, polygamy, and sexual slavery are approved of under the ever watchful eye of the God of the Bible.

Chapter A6: Religions Are Grandfathered Cults

Ancient religions survive under the discriminatory and prejudicial protection of governments worldwide. Religions are basically grandfathered cults with special protections.

If we were to grant the argument, in favor of religion, that faith alone is enough to believe in a religion, and that evidence of that belief is not required, then there is an unlimited number of beliefs that people could apply for; in terms of starting a new, recognized religion. If your only argument in favor of your religion is "faith," and not any evidence; then what is to stop other people from making whatever religions they want based solely on their faith.

These religions would only be limited by the imagination of the person starting this new religion. **Luckily, we have evidence of what happens when people try to start new religions. These new startup religions are pejoratively called "Cults," and persecuted under existing government law. They are not given any special protections, or privileges, based on faith alone. This is obviously discriminatory.**

Interestingly, the same thing happened to ancient religions at the time that they were newly proposed. Jesus and earlier Christians were persecuted for their beliefs at the time that Christianity was in its nascent stage. **Again, this shows that there is nothing special about older religions, except that they have had hundreds of years to accumulate and gather billions of followers.**

A detailed examination of modern and recent cults is beyond the scope of this book. However, if the reader was so inclined, there are many examples of cults, and what happened to them that the reader could look up and research. These include: (a) **Warren Jeffs** and the Fundamentalist Church of Jesus Christ of Latter Day Saints: <u>Jeffs was sentenced to life in prison plus 20 years for charges that included incest, which is essentially the same conduct that makes up the Bible's Genesis narrative</u>; (b) **Heaven's Gate** cult; (c) **David Koresh** and the Branch Davidians, and many more.

Similarly, certain scientific disciplines seemingly bow down and give special privilege to grandfathered religions. For example, in psychiatry, the definition of a delusion is a "fixed belief that is not amenable to change in light of conflicting evidence." However, psychiatry subtly suggests that religious background must be taken into account in evaluating a delusional disorder, which conceivably results in the often repeated statement, "When one person has a fixed, false belief, it is a delusion; when many do, it is a religion."

This, of course, conveniently excludes older, established religions from being examined as a fixed, false, belief;

while the newer, startup religions, the so–called cults, get no protections. That is not really very scientific. Such is the discriminatory power that older, established religions hold over the world today.

Imagine, if today, a group of people claiming to practice a new religion tried to publish stories suggesting that the human race has descended from people committing all kinds of incest: brother-sister incest, father-daughter incest, and so on, what would happen?

All manner of law-enforcement agencies would likely get mobilized, and people would refer to the practitioners of such a belief system as a cult. Yet, for 2000 years, the Bible has published exactly these, and other outlandish stories, and no less than 2.2 billion people seem to be under its influence. The only sensible explanation must be that most of these people have not read through the Bible themselves, or are not aware of these abhorrent stories. We shall examine some of these stories further in **Section B: Biblical Christianity v/s Modern U.S. and Western Culture**.

Regardless of whether you are a believer of Christianity, Islam, Judaism, or Hinduism; the fact is that the majority of the Earth's population does not believe in your particular religion. That means that there is not one religion on Earth that the majority of the Earth's population believes in. Furthermore, anyone who studies these religions closely will note that these religions are mutually exclusive of each other.

These days, some people tend to say, for example, "I am a Christian, but I believe in Hinduism as well," or vice versa, or that "all religions speak the truth." These folks have actually not closely studied any religion. <u>This is an example of a synthetic delusion</u>. If you believe in Christianity, you cannot then believe in Hinduism, or Islam. Each religion clearly identifies all other Gods and religions to be false.

<u>Synthetic delusions are those that are combined, or synthesized, out of one or more primary delusions, such as the primary delusion of the existence of God.</u> An example of this is when people try to synthesize different religions into whatever fantasy suits them, such as saying that all religions are basically the same path to spirituality, or some other similar sounding nonsense, without understanding that most religions specifically forbid other religious doctrines.

Obviously, that prima facie poses a dilemma. All cannot be true based on the clear writings in their respective holy books as shown below:

It is self-evident that the polytheistic gods of Hinduism, v/s Jesus, v/s Mohammed, cannot all be valid, and true. Bottom line is: Muslims believe in Mohammed as the last prophet, while Christians, Hindus and Jews don't. Christians believe in Jesus as the son of God, while Jews and Hindus don't. Hindus believe in multiple Gods (Shiva, Krishna, Brahma, Rama), while Jews, Christians, and Muslims don't. Jews don't believe in the divinity of any of the above, whether it be Jesus, Mohammed, or the pantheon of Hindu Gods.

Therefore, a lot of what goes on in the modern world today, is basically one very large group of delusional people trying to tolerate the delusions of another very large group of people, in return for the same favor. Sometimes, this tolerance succeeds; at other times, it does not. More often than not, you get one group of delusional people trying to blow up a different group of delusional people, and succeeding at it.

Chapter A7: Most People Don't Really Believe In God

People who say that they believe in the Bible are flat out stretching the truth. Logically speaking, how or why would you believe in something that promises to send you to hell for the things that you are doing? As has been shown in **Chapter A4** under **(9) Psychological bribing**, the chances of anyone entering the fictional Biblical heaven are essentially zero. Please review that portion of the book for more details.

The proof that most religious people don't really believe in their religion, or God, is that these people do not really follow all the tenets of the religion that they're supposed to believe in. In the case of Christianity, <u>if you are rich and do not give away ALL of your possessions to the poor, or if you have premarital sex, or if you divorce and remarry, and numerous other things; you are going against the teachings of the Bible, and therefore, cannot go into heaven</u>.

The above shows that most people don't really believe that God exists, or they haven't given it much thought. They go along with society, or with their family, or friends, to church and temples as part of ordinary life, but probably don't spend much time analyzing it. People are too busy making ends meet, completing their household chores, taking care of their children, getting their work done, socializing, and entertaining, to give it much thought.

IF JESUS WERE TO RETURN:

Some people say that they're waiting for Jesus to return. However, if you think about it carefully, we already have a very good idea of what Jesus would say if he were to return. Let us consider the following situation:

If you truly believe that the Bible is the inerrant and infallible word of God, and you believe that the teachings of Jesus do not change, then we already know what Jesus would say, if, or when, he returns. Let us consider the issue of wealth and money, for example. The teachings of Jesus are very clear on this issue, in multiple verses, in the New Testament. Please refer to **Chapter B8: Giving money to the poor** for details.

To those people who are waiting for Jesus to return, and who believe in the infallibility of the Bible, it should be very clear that Jesus would say **(Chapter B8)**: (a) sell all your belongings, and give the money to the poor; (b) do not store treasures upon the Earth; (c) it is easier for a camel to go through the eye of a needle than for someone who is rich to enter the kingdom of God.

Therefore, Jesus would be very disappointed at all the wealth that most Americans have built-up and stored for themselves. What are we to make of this? There are only a few possibilities:

(a) modern Christians do not know what Jesus says in the Bible regarding riches and money.

(b) modern Christians do not really believe the Bible is the true word of God or Jesus; in which case, they are not really Christians.

(c) modern Christians are ignoring the teachings of Jesus; in which case, they are not really Christians.

If they do not know what Jesus says in the Bible, they are demonstrating a very high level of ignorance. If they really don't believe that the Bible is the true word of God, or Jesus, then that just proves that they aren't really Christians. If they are just ignoring the teachings of Jesus, then again they are not Christians.

Therefore, the only way modern Christians can explain away the reason that they are not following the teachings of Jesus is by claiming ignorance. This "ignorance" explanation would be really very far-fetched, and self-serving. It is a more reasonable explanation that modern Christians don't really believe in the authenticity of the Bible, or the teachings of Jesus; hence, this proves that they are not really Christians, nor do they believe in a Biblical God.

In the 2007 American movie, "Evan Almighty," God comes and speaks directly to congressman Evan Baxter, played by the actor Steve Carell. However, Evan is very reluctant to mention that God is communicating and speaking with him to build an Ark. Even most of the people around him are very concerned that he should not mention any of this to the general public, or his other congressmen colleagues that God has been speaking to him.

Why, might one ask, if the majority of people really believed that God exists, then why would it be so bad for anyone to find out that you were speaking with him? This shows the double standard in society whereby it is OK for everybody to make passing references to God, but heaven forbid (pun intended), if God actually starts speaking to you, then all hell (pun intended), breaks loose.

<u>This is proof, that deep down, people don't really believe in God. If they did, they would start to rejoice and celebrate, if they found that God was speaking to anyone. Instead, if a person were to claim that God is speaking to him; he, or she, is likely to be ridiculed, mocked, persecuted, laughed at, and likely to be put in a mental institution.</u>

Religion therefore, is analogous to joining a country club, or golf club of some sort. To join a country club, you have to pay a fee. Going to church and participating in, and benefiting from the social connectivity that happens there is analogous to going to a club. However, in this case, the ticket, or fee to enter this club is that you have to believe, or pretend to believe, in a delusion.

Chapter A8: The Superstitions Of Jesus

I n **Chapter A2: Evidence against a Biblical God**, and other chapters, it was shown without a shadow of doubt that the Bible is the work of primitive peasants, not of a God, nor could it be inspired by a God. Here, we will look at the many superstitions that the Bible attributes to Jesus, and arrive at the same conclusion.

In their zeal to make Jesus out to be divine in nature, the authors of the Bible attributed many miracles to him in The New Testament. However, they did not do themselves any favors by doing so. Whether we choose to believe that Jesus actually performed these miracles (that is we interpret these passages literally), or we believe that these were just made up stories; in either case, the lack of any divine spark or knowledge, is pretty clear in these passages. Let us look at them in more detail and see why:

(1) The Bible attributes Jesus as thinking leprosy is caused by being unclean:

Matthew 8:1-4

When Jesus came down from the mountainside, large crowds followed him. A man with leprosy came and knelt before him and said, "Lord, if you are willing, you can make me clean."

Jesus reached out his hand and touched the man. "I am willing," he said. "Be clean!" Immediately he was cleaned of his leprosy.

Then Jesus said to him, "see that you don't tell anyone. But go, show yourself to the priest and offer the gift Moses commanded, as a testimony to them."

FACT CHECK: Leprosy is caused by the bacteria *Mycobacterium Leprae* or *Mycobacterium Lepromatosis*. Treatment is with various medications which may include *dapsone, rifampicin, clofazimine* or other medications. In the past 20 years, 16 million people worldwide have been cured of leprosy. Leprosy is not considered very contagious. However, transmission to close contacts does occur. The mode of transmission is thought to be by cough, or nasal droplets. The Bible mentions none of the above facts in the relevant verses: whether it be the mechanism of disease, or patho-physiology of leprosy, or it's treatment.

RATIONALIZATIONS:

We sometimes hear these rubbish rationalizations over and over again: that (a) the Bible has to be understood in the context of the bronze age 2000 years ago, and (b) that the Bible is a spiritual text, not a scientific one. These are self-defeating, rubbish rationalizations as will be shown below.

Firstly, if something was inspired by God, or written by God, as so many priests and biblical scholars proclaim about the Bible, it would be timeless and ageless. It would be as valid today as it was 2000 years ago, and still be as valid 2000 years in the future from today.

So, these priests and scholars are themselves using a self-defeating argument. Because, if they're claiming that the Bible is only valid in a 2000 year old context, then they have admitted that it is a useless piece of writing for modern humans.

Secondly, one might ask the following question: if the Biblical God could make ancient Biblical people live to be 950 years old, then why couldn't he also give them enough of a modern brain to understand at least basic biology, physics, chemistry, microbiology, or pathology, just to give a few examples?

In *__Genesis 9:29__*, it says:

Noah lived a total of 950 years, and then he died.

Remember that the Bible is full of examples of these early Biblical primitives living for hundreds of years. Imagine the ludicrousness of the rationalization that the Biblical God could not give these primitives a modern brain, but could make them live to be 950 years old. What does it say about a God who would much rather interact for 950 years with a primitive goat herder, rather than create smart, intelligent humans with whom to interact?

It is obvious that it is not a genius God or creator that created humans; otherwise, in addition to living 950 years, these early humans would also have had a very smart, intelligent brain; and they would have lived in a peaceful, utopian, modern society; not one in which they had to run around naked in a garden listening to a talking snake, like sub-human pets.

Therefore, it is a highly incongruous and ludicrous rationalization to suggest that the Biblical God was able to make these early primitives live for hundreds of years, but not give them a basic knowledge of physics, chemistry, biology, pathology, microbiology, or the germ theory of diseases. Let us review some more superstitions attributable to Jesus:

(2) The Bible attributes Jesus as thinking that paralysis is caused by sin:

Matthew 9:1-7

Jesus stepped into a boat, crossed over and came to his own town. Some men brought to him a paralyzed man, lying on a mat.

When Jesus saw their faith, he said to the man, "Take heart, son; your sins are forgiven." .....

.....So he said to the paralyzed man, "get up, take your mat and go home." Then the man got up and went home.

FACT CHECK: Paralysis is a loss of muscle function for one or more muscles. It is most often caused by damage in the nervous system, whether the brain, or spinal cord. There are many causes including, but not limited to: *stroke, multiple sclerosis, polio, injury,* and so on. *Drugs* or *toxins* can also cause paralysis. <u>There is absolutely no evidence to suggest that sinners are being struck down disproportionately by paralysis.</u>

(3) The Bible attributes Jesus as thinking that being mute is caused by demons:

Matthew 9:32-33

While they were going out, a man who was demon-possessed and could not talk was brought to Jesus. And when the demon was driven out, the man who had been mute spoke.

FACT CHECK: Muteness is an inability to speak. It may be caused by problems with the *esophagus, vocal cords, tongue* or other body parts involved in the speech process. Injury to certain areas of the brain such as the *Broca's* area can also cause muteness. <u>There is absolutely no evidence to suggest that demons are involved in causing muteness.</u>

Section B: Biblical Christianity v/s Modern U.S. and Western Culture

Introduction To Section B:

I went to Christian schools throughout my entire childhood. Starting in nursery or kindergarten, all the way to the end of high school, my entire education was in Christian schools. This included schools run by Catholic sisters, by the Patrician Brothers, and other Christian schools that give me a good, though sanitized grasp of Christianity. I thoroughly enjoyed academic and sports activities in these schools, as well as learning some Christian theology, and singing Christian hymns and songs.

There is a huge disconnect between what most modern Christians believe today, and what is actually written in the Bible. Most Christians today have not even carefully read the first five books of the Old Testament (Genesis, Exodus, Leviticus, Numbers and Deuteronomy), or the first four books of the New Testament (Matthew, Mark, Luke and John).

A careful reading of just these nine books, which encompass just a small part of the Bible should be an essential prerequisite to becoming a Christian, one would think. For, on what basis does one call himself or herself a Christian if one does not know what being a Christian is all about?

Most people get their information about the Bible secondhand from someone else. This, of course, is a huge mistake. How can you be a good doctor if you haven't read and understood all the relevant medical textbooks? How can you be a good lawyer if you haven't read and understood all the relevant law books? Similarly, how would you know what being a Christian entails, without having personally read and understood all the relevant books in the Bible.

I heard a pastor claim recently on the TV that 3.9 billion people had read the Bible. He was basing this off some statistics that 3.9 billion Bibles had been sold. Unfortunately, it is self-evident that not many of these people who brought these Bibles, or were given these Bibles actually read through them.

The evidence is that I have not heard any large-scale, or for that matter small-scale discussion about so many topics in the Bible that would be considered very relevant for discussion today in the modern world. If 3.9 billion people actually read the Bible and understood it, or even 1 million people read and understood it; I would expect there to be a tsunami of massive proportions of people dying to discuss it everywhere, whether in print, or on social media, or anyplace else that one expects a discussion these days.

The reason for this is that if you actually read the Bible, you will find that it has become obsolete. You can pick up any topic you want from the Bible, whether it is homosexuality, adultery, incest, status of women, slavery, rights of the disabled, and other topics that we will discuss in more detail in this book, and you will find a common thread.

The common thread is that most, if not all modern Christians no longer believe in the laws or guidelines that are espoused clearly in the Bible with regard to the above issues. Most modern Christians believe men and women are equal, that disabled people have rights, that slavery is wrong, that homosexuals do not deserve to be punished by death, that a woman does not deserve to be stoned to death if she's not a virgin at the time of marriage, and so on.

Despite all this, the Bible teaches quite the opposite. Biblical Christianity involves discriminating against the disabled, discriminating against women and children, stoning women if they are not virgins at the time of marriage, propagating slavery, putting homosexuals to death, and a lot of other things that have fallen into the trash heap of history at the time of this writing.

So, what does it mean to be a modern Christian? If you believe the Bible, you cannot be a Christian unless you follow every letter, or particle of the letter written in the Bible. This disqualifies almost every modern Christian from calling himself or herself a Christian, because no modern Christian that I know of would believe in every letter written in the Bible.

Jesus is attributed as saying in **_Matthew 5:17-19:_**

"Do not think that I have come to abolish the law or the Prophets. I have not come to abolish them but to fulfill them. For truly I tell you, until heaven and earth disappear, not the smallest letter, not the least stroke of a pen, will by any means disappear from the law until everything is accomplished. Therefore anyone who sets aside one of the least of these Commands and teaches others accordingly will be called least in the kingdom of heaven.

Therefore, even Jesus is pretty clear on this issue. If you are to be a Christian, you have to follow every letter of the law in the Bible. Modern Christians run into this problem. If there is something they don't like in the Biblical passages, they either rationalize it by saying that it is an Old Testament issue, and does not apply to them; or that they don't believe in the particular passages in question, and that they only pick and choose the "good" passages.

However, as shown in **_Matthew 5:17-19_** above, a Christian cannot really pick and choose passages from the Bible, but is obligated to follow every letter in it. Therefore, according to Jesus himself, as a good Christian, it is your duty to familiarize yourself with all of the Bible, and follow it.

It was not until later in my life that I started reading the Bible with great depth and intensity. To my horror, instead of being drawn closer to Christianity as I had hoped would happen, **I began discovering verses that bought me to an inescapable conclusion: The Bible could not be the word of God.**

I read and reread these verses, and read other parts of the Bible as well. Each time, I came closer to the realization that I had discovered something. The issue of whether the Bible is, or is not the word of God, has at the time of this writing, become an irrelevant issue to some extent, because in modern Western culture, our modern governments through their legislatures and courts have already enacted laws, and come to decisions that have made the Bible completely obsolete.

Modern laws and decisions in the United States, United Kingdom, and other countries are in complete opposition to Biblical laws and guidelines. This again supports the conclusion that the Bible isn't really the word of God. The facts are crystal clear. **On every topic, such as homosexuality, adultery, slavery, gender discrimination, disabled persons rights, and other topics, the Bible is on the wrong side of history.**

Therefore, I began writing this section which examines Biblical laws on critical topics, and examines the corresponding modern laws on those same topics, and shows how the values of these United States (or of other modern Western governments), are not consistent with the values espoused in the Bible. **Therefore, we can now show, with complete certainty and without any reasonable doubt, that Biblical laws and guidelines are obsolete.**

Let us now examine specific Biblical laws / guidelines, and the corresponding modern laws in western culture (<u>taking the United States as the primary example</u>), on each of the topics below. These will be divided into the following ten chapters:

Chapter B1: Homosexuality

FACT: The United States does not put homosexuals to death as preached in the Bible.

The fate of homosexuals is made very clear in the Bible, both in the Old Testament, and in the New Testament. The Old Testament passages below are derived from Leviticus, and the New Testament passages below are derived from Romans, and 1 Corinthians:

Leviticus 20:13

"if a man has sexual relations with a man as one does with a woman, both of them have done what is detestable. They are to be put to death; their blood will be on their own heads."

The message is very clear. Homosexuality is punishable by death without fail.

Leviticus 18:22

"Do not have sexual relations with a man as one does with a woman; that is detestable."

Romans 1:26-27; 32

"Because of this, God gave them over to shameful lusts. Even their women exchanged natural sexual relations for unnatural ones. In the same way, the men also abandoned natural relations with women and were inflamed with lust for one another...... Although they know God's righteous decree that those who do such things deserve death, they not only continue to do these very things but also approve of those who practice them."

In other words, in the Romans passages, homosexuality is seen as a punishment from God, wherein males become lustful towards males just as females have gone against nature; even though they know that the punishment for homosexuality is death.

1 Corinthians 6:9-10

"Or do you not know that wrongdoers will not inherit the kingdom of God? Do not be deceived: Neither the sexually immoral nor idolaters nor adulterers nor men who have sex with men, nor thieves nor the greedy persons nor drunkards nor slanderers nor swindlers will inherit the kingdom of God."

HOMOSEXUALITY IN MODERN UNITED STATES CULTURE:

Same-sex sexual activity between consenting adults of the same sex has been legal nationwide in the United States of America since June 26, 2003, pursuant to the U.S. Supreme Court ruling in Lawrence v. Texas. Furthermore, as of June

26, 2015, <u>all states license and recognize marriage between</u> <u>same-sex couples</u> as a result of the Supreme Court's decision in Obergefell v. Hodges.

<u>Adoption of children by same-sex married couples is also</u> <u>legal nationwide</u> since the June 2015 decision above; with the exception of Mississippi which did not have its same-sex adoption ban struck down by a federal court until March 2016.

In Lawrence v. Texas, the United States Supreme Court struck down the sodomy law in Texas in a 6-3 decision and, by extension, invalidated sodomy laws in 13 other states, making same-sex sexual activity legal in every U.S. state and territory. The court held that intimate consensual sexual conduct was part of the liberty protected by substantive due process under the 14th amendment to the Constitution.

As of 1960, every state had an anti-sodomy law. At that time, most judges were largely unsympathetic to the substantive due process claims raised. However, 43 years later, in 2003, all that had changed. Then, in 2015, under Obergefell v. Hodges, the Supreme Court of the United States ruled that the fundamental right to marry is guaranteed to same-sex couples by both the due process clause and the equal protection clause of the 14th amendment to the United States Constitution.

This ruling meant that all 50 states must lawfully perform and recognize the marriages of same-sex couples on the same terms and conditions as the marriages of opposite sex couples, with all the accompanying rights and responsibilities.

FINAL ANALYSIS AND CONCLUSION:

The Bible appears to be on the wrong side of history on the issue of homosexuality. While Biblical Christianity explicitly states that the penalty for homosexuality is death; all 50 states in the United States allow for homosexual activity between consenting adults, allow and recognize marriages between same-sex couples, as well as allow same-sex married couples to adopt children.

The contradiction between Biblical Christianity and modern United States culture on the issue of homosexuality could not be more glaring. Today, most people calling themselves Christians do not have a problem with same-sex couples marrying or adopting children, or being in a relationship, despite this being a specific prohibition punishable by death in the Bible.

Therefore, they follow a socio-cultural concept of Christianity developed over just the past few decades, and not the Biblical concept of Christianity. Per ***Mathew 5:17-19*** as discussed before, they are not Biblical Christians, and cannot enter the Kingdom of heaven of the Biblical God.

Furthermore, if God really existed as described in the Bible, and the Bible was his word, we would expect that countries that have openly accepted gays and lesbians into the mainstream, and openly accepted same-sex marriage;

would be punished and would become terrible places to live in. In the Bible, it says that homosexuals are to be put to death immediately.

However, we see quite the opposite happening. Indeed, countries in which gays and lesbians are still repressed also seem to be the countries where life is still pretty horrible. In fact, it is the liberal advanced Western democracies of the world that legalized gay marriage which are still the best places to live in the world. <u>Therefore, it is obvious that the Bible is absolutely false on this count, and the Biblical God is a piece of ancient, obsolete, irrelevant fiction.</u>

Chapter B2: Adultery

FACT: The United States does not condemn people to death for adultery as preached in the Bible.

Both the Old Testament and the New Testament have laws forbidding adultery. The Old Testament passages include the one below from *Leviticus*, while the New Testament passages include the passages from *Matthew* and *Mark* below:

Leviticus 20:10

If a man commits adultery with another man's wife - with the wife of his neighbor - both the adulterer and the adulteress are to be put to death.

Matthew 5:27-28

You have heard that it was said 'you shall not commit adultery.' But I tell you that anyone who looks at a woman lustfully has already committed adultery with her in his heart.

Matthew 5:31-32

It has been said, 'anyone who divorces his wife must give her a certificate of divorce.' But I tell you that anyone who divorces *his wife, except for sexual immorality, makes her the victim of adultery, and <u>anyone who marries a divorced woman commits adultery</u>.*

Mark 10:11-12

<u>"Anyone who divorces his wife and marries another woman commits adultery against her. And if she divorces her husband and marries another man, she commits adultery."</u>

So, essentially, if you believe in the God of the Bible, and you have been divorced and remarried, you have committed the sin of adultery, punishable by death. Essentially, what this means is that there is probably a very small minuscule minority of population in the United States or Western culture, or even in the whole world, who would qualify to go into heaven based on these and other verses in the Bible.

If the imaginary God of your mind is different and allows you to be rich, and allows you to be remarried, then that is incompatible and inconsistent with the God of the Bible. The messages above are crystal clear. Adultery is punishable by death. If you marry a divorced woman, you are committing adultery. You are committing adultery merely by looking at a woman in a sexualized manner.

Considering that in the modern world, people are bombarded on a daily basis with sexualized pictures of women in the media, magazines, movies, and other forms of social media, this puts the entire population of the

modern world at risk for adultery, and therefore, at risk of the penalty of death if Biblical guidelines were in effect.

The New Testament says that if you marry a divorced woman, you are committing adultery. What is the percentage of population in the United States, or the rest of the modern world who have married a divorced woman? This puts a considerable number of people as having violated the Biblical law of adultery, and at risk of the penalty of death.

Interestingly, so many of our leaders or politicians who call themselves Christians have committed adultery according to Biblical guidelines. How many politicians come to mind who have had affairs, or were divorced and remarried? All are guilty of adultery if Biblical guidelines were in effect.

Even in England, Kings and Queens have found themselves in situations where they were running afoul of the Bible. This led to some very interesting stories and developments, including how the current royal family in England accidentally came into power. Here are those stories:

The story of King Edward VIII:

It is important to recognize just how much power the Bible has wielded over even Kings and Queens for hundreds of years. In January 1936, King Edward VIII took over as King of the United Kingdom, and the dominions of the British Empire upon the death of his father, King George V. Only months into his reign, he created a constitutional crisis by proposing marriage to Wallis Simpson, an American who had divorced her first husband, and was seeking a divorce from her second.

Such a marriage would have conflicted with Edward's status as the titular head of the church of England, which at that time disapproved of remarriage after divorce if a former spouse was still alive. When it became apparent that he could not marry Wallis and remain on the throne, Edward abdicated in December 1936. With a reign of less than a year, he was one of the shortest reigning monarchs in British history.

This abdication resulted in his younger brother George VI becoming King of the United Kingdom. This changed the line of succession from Edward's children to those of his brother George VI. Thereafter, George VI's daughter Elizabeth II became Queen of the United Kingdom in 1952, and she is still currently the longest reigning monarch as of the time of this writing.

The story of Henry VIII:

Centuries before this, it was Henry VIII who came into disagreement with the Pope on the question of annulment of his first marriage to Catherine of Aragon. This prompted him to initiate the English Reformation, separating the Church of England from papal authority in 1534. He appointed himself the supreme head of the Church of England, and dissolved convents and monasteries.

Despite his resulting excommunication, Henry VIII remained a believer in core Catholic theological teachings. This did not prevent him from marrying six times, and executing two of his wives, Anne Boleyn, and Catherine Howard, for adultery. A dramatized account of the fate of Anne Boleyn was released as the motion picture "The Other Boleyn Girl," in 2008. **How interesting, that he did not have himself executed as well, for the sin of adultery, considering that he divorced and remarried so many times, in flagrant violation of the Bible.**

ADULTERY IN MODERN WESTERN CULTURE:

We have come a long way since then. In July 2002, the Church of England gave its overwhelming official backing for divorced couples to remarry in church, removing a symbolic obstacle in the way of Prince Charles marrying Camilla Parker Bowles. In a victory for liberals, it's ruling body, the General Synod voted by 269 votes to 83 in favor of ending a dilemma that had afflicted the church from its earliest days.

In 2005, Prince Charles and Camilla Parker Bowles, both having been divorced previously, married under these new rules, without Prince Charles having to give up his title as the heir apparent, and next in line to the British throne. More history was made on May 19, 2018 after the marriage of Prince Harry and Meghan Markle at St. George's Chapel, Windsor castle. Ms. Markle had been divorced previously as well. <u>Under actual Biblical rules, both Prince Charles and Prince Harry, as well as Camilla and Meghan Markle would be guilty of adultery.</u>

As is fairly evident from all of the above, Biblical guidelines and rules have slowly been chipped away in modern western culture. At the time of this writing, most of the Biblical guidelines on the topic of adultery are obsolete. Unfortunately, for King Edward VIII, in January 1936, all of these changes came too late. He was unable to avoid his fate, and had to give up the throne as detailed above, resulting in his brother George VI becoming King of the United Kingdom. This changed the line of succession from Edward's children to those of George VI which includes the current Monarch Queen Elizabeth II, her son Prince Charles, and grandson Prince William.

The United States is still one of the few industrialized countries to still have laws criminalizing adultery, though none of these laws involves punishment by death. In the United States, laws vary from state to state. These laws have gradually been abolished, or struck down by courts as unconstitutional. Pennsylvania abolished its fornication and adultery laws in 1973. In recent years, West Virginia repealed their adultery laws in 2010, Colorado in 2013 and New Hampshire in 2014.

FINAL ANALYSIS AND CONCLUSION:

The Bible appears to be on the wrong side of history on the issue of adultery as well. In most modern western countries, there are no longer any prohibitions on getting divorced, on getting remarried, or on marrying divorced people. These actions are not considered adultery in modern Western culture. Nor is any form of adultery punishable by death as the Bible decrees. Again, we see that many people calling themselves Christians that live in these countries, do not actually follow Biblical laws, while continuing to call themselves Christians.

Chapter B3: Virginity Of Women

FACT: The United States does not stone women to death who are not Virgins at the time of marriage.

The following are the Bible's laws on the status of women at the time of marriage. The passages start with:

Deuteronomy 22:13

If a man takes a wife and after sleeping with her,...

and end with:

Deuteronomy 22:20-21

"*If, however, the charge is true and no proof of the young woman's virginity can be found, she shall be brought to the door of her father's house and there the men of her town shall stone her to death....*"

FINAL ANALYSIS AND CONCLUSION:

The meaning of the above Biblical passage is crystal clear. If a woman is found not to be a virgin at the time of her marriage, she must be killed by stoning at the entrance

of her father's house. Incidentally, no such passages exist for men at the time of marriage, showing the gender discrimination prevalent in the Bible.

It is self-evident, that in modern Western culture, we do not stone women to death for not being virgins at the time of marriage. The Bible again proves to be on the wrong side of history on this issue as well.

Some priests, or Biblical scholars may want to say that there is substantially more forgiveness in The New Testament. There is the story of Jesus forgiving a woman caught in adultery in an indirect manner in _**John 8:1-11**_ by saying, _"Let any one of you who is without sin be the first to throw a stone at her."_

However, I refer you back to Jesus, who is attributed as saying in _**Matthew 5:17-19:**_

"Do not think that I have come to abolish the law or the Prophets. I have not come to abolish them but to fulfill them. For truly I tell you, until heaven and earth disappear, not the smallest letter, not the least stroke of a pen, will by any means disappear from the law until everything is accomplished. Therefore anyone who sets aside one of the least of these Commands and teaches others accordingly will be called least in the kingdom of heaven.

Jesus himself says that anyone who tries to set aside any of the Biblical guidelines from The Old Testament, and teaches others accordingly, will be called least in the kingdom of heaven. Obviously, this means that Jesus himself cannot set aside any of The Old Testament guidelines. Therefore, though he succeeds in circumventing The Old Testament, he does so by contradicting himself in **_Matthew 5:17-19_**. Furthermore, he neglects to address the real issue of whether it is moral, or ethical to stone a woman to death.

Modern western culture leaves no such ambiguity on this issue. It is patently clear in modern western culture that it is illegal, immoral, and unethical to stone anyone to death for what they do in their own private life.

Chapter B4: Incest And Other Sexual Escapades

FACT: **The United States does not condone incest. It prosecutes people engaged in incest.**

However, in direct contradiction of the above, the very essence of the Bible narrative of the propagation of the human race in Genesis depends heavily on Incest. This has already been dealt with in an introductory manner in the **Chapter A5 on Creationism** earlier. We will explore it some more here:

PART 1: **INCEST AND OTHER SEXUAL BEHAVIOR SANCTIONED BY THE BIBLICAL GOD**

Judah has sex with his daughter-in-law, Tamar, and produces Perez, who is a direct ancestor of Joseph, husband of Mary, mother to Jesus:

Genesis 38:15-19

When Judah saw her, he thought she was a prostitute, for she had covered her face. Not realizing that she was his daughter-in-law, he went over to her by the roadside and said, "Come now, let me sleep with you."

"And what will you give me to sleep with you?" she asked.

"I'll send you a young goat from my flock," he said.

"Will you give me something as a pledge until you send it?" she asked.

He said "What pledge should I give you?"

"Your seal and its cord, and the staff in your hand," she answered.

<u>*So he gave them to her and slept with her, and she became pregnant by him.*</u>

Thereafter, he is about to burn his daughter-in-law for prostitution, when she makes it known to him that it was he who impregnated her.

<u>**Genesis 38:24-26**</u>

About three months later Judah was told, "Your daughter-in-law is guilty of prostitution, and as a result she is now pregnant."

Judah said "Bring her out and have her be burned to death!"

As she was being brought out, she sent a message to her father-in-law. "I am pregnant by the man who owns these," she said. And she added, "See if you recognize whose seal and cord and staff these are."

"Judah recognized them and said, "She is more righteous than I, since I wouldn't give her to my son Shelah." And he did not sleep with her again.

This brazen episode ends with Tamar giving birth to twins, called Perez, and Zerah, in *Genesis 38:27-30*;

As above, it is noted in the Bible that Judah has sex with his daughter-in-law, and has children resulting in one of the children being the direct forefather of Joseph, who is married to Mary, who gives birth to Jesus. Thus, those that do have sex even with their daughter-in-law are spared, and even given high privilege like Judah as evidenced in *Matthew 1:3* "Judah became father to Perez..."

Matthew 1:1-16 essentially traces the lineage from Abraham, to Isaac, to Jacob, to Judah, to Perez, to Hezron, and finally ending with *"Joseph the husband of Mary, of whom Jesus was born, who is also called Christ."* Therefore the Bible in *Matthew 1:1-16* plainly and very clearly indicates that Joseph's ancestors came directly from copulation of Judah and his daughter-in-law Tamar, through their progeny Perez. Thus, Judah is exalted in spite of having had sinful sex with his daughter-in-law.

On the other hand, those like Onan, who refuse to have sex or children within the family, are in fact put to death by the Biblical God as evidenced in *Genesis 38:8-10*

Then Judah said to Onan, "Sleep with your brother's wife and fulfill your duty to her as a brother-in-law to raise up offspring for your brother."

But Onan knew that the child would not be his; so whenever he slept with his brother's wife, he spilled his semen on the ground to keep from providing offspring for his brother. What he did was wicked in the LORD's sight; so the LORD put him to death also.

ANALYSIS:

This whole episode shows just how highly incongruent different parts of the Bible are. In some parts of the Bible, fornication and adultery are punishable by death. Yet, in Genesis, there are many stories of not just fornication and adultery, but also incest and polygamy that don't lead to any punishment, but may actually lead to reward. This proves that the Bible is not the word of an all-knowing, all-powerful God, but of humans who did not even have the common sense, or means, to check their stories with each other to give consistency to the Bible. Let's discuss these contradictions in further detail.

PART 2: SEXUAL CONTRADICTIONS IN THE BIBLE

The contradictions in the Bible on the subject of sex and incest are so astounding that it is proof itself that the Bible is not the word of God, but the word of babbling, confused, bronze age humans that a reasonable person would assume were probably too drunk to remember what they were writing, with the result that they keep on

contradicting themselves, within the same Bible, within the same Testament on the same topics.

Let us take specific examples of what the Bible says and compare the Genesis stories earlier in this Chapter with what is written in ***Leviticus 18:7-18***:

Leviticus 18:7

Do not dishonor your father by having sexual relations with your mother.

Other Biblical translations make it clear that neither sex with your father or mother are permitted.

Leviticus 18:9

Do not have sexual relations with your sister.

Leviticus 18:15

Do not have sexual relations with your daughter-in-law.

Leviticus 18:18

Do not take your wife's sister as a rival wife and have sexual relations with her while your wife is living.

ANALYSIS:

Therefore, in ***Leviticus 18:6–18***, there are *judicial decisions* that God says must be kept, including, but not limited to, not having sex with your father, not having sex with your daughter-in-law, and not having sex with two sisters while both are still alive.

However, this directly contradicts other accounts presented earlier in the Bible in which father-daughter sex occurs (Lot and his daughters), sex with a daughter-in-law occurs (Judah and Tamar), and sex occurs with two sisters while both are still alive (Jacob with sisters Leah and Rachel, both also his cousins).

The relevant passages (discussed in detail elsewhere) are:

Genesis 29:15-35 in which Jacob marries and has sexual relations with two sisters, Leah and Rachel, who incidentally also happen to be his cousins. He is married to both AND their respective slave girls all at the same time.

Genesis 19:32-38 in which Lots' two daughters both have sex with their father and produce offspring with him, essentially raping him in the process, by first making him unconscious with wine.

Genesis 38:15-30 in which Judah has sex with his daughter-in-law and produces children, one of whom is the direct ancestor of Joseph, husband of Mary, who was mother of Jesus.

Imagine the most glaring of all possible contradictions: that the husband of Mary, who is the mother of Jesus, is actually a product of forbidden, sinful sex between Judah

<u>and his daughter-in-law Tamar, something which is directly</u> <u>forbidden by God as discussed above in *Leviticus 18:15*</u>

FINAL ANALYSIS AND CONCLUSION:

How are such glaring contradictions possible?

The word of God in *Leviticus 18:15* specifically forbids sex between father-in-law and daughter-in-law. However, it is this exact sexual relationship between Judah and his daughter-in-law Tamar that gives rise to twins, one of whom is Perez, who is the direct ancestor of Joseph, who is married to Mary, who gives birth to Jesus.

Why did God not strike down Judah's descendants due to Judah having broken God's decisions by having sex with his daughter-in-law Tamar?

Instead, how do those descendants of Judah from an improper, illegal, and sinful (in God's eye) relationship ultimately end up leading right to Joseph who has the high exalted position of being the foster father, or stepfather if you will, of Jesus himself?

These are just some of the glaring discrepancies in the narrative of the Bible. The only reasonable or logical explanations, or conclusions, are that the Bible is the work of different human authors with absolutely no divine revelation, who did not check in with each other to make sure that their work was consistent with each other,

or the work of one author who was too drunk to keep his stories consistent.

Despite all of the above mountain of evidence garnered from the Bible itself, if there is still someone who would like to keep on believing that the Bible is indeed the word of God, then the fact remains that the word is glaringly inconsistent, and incompatible, on a very huge and dramatic scale. An all-powerful, all-knowing, wise God could never have such an inconsistent and incongruent description of rules, or application of rules. Hence, if it is the word of God, it is the work of a very imperfect and confused God. Since the God of our imagination is neither imperfect or confused, it follows that our initial conclusions that the Bible is the work of bronze age humans with nary a divine spark must stand as the correct conclusion.

Recently, I was reading an explanation given by some religious website that attempts to explain away the above contradictions. The author of this explanation purports to say that incest was legal in the beginning of the Bible, such as in Genesis; however, that God made it illegal in later books of the Bible. This rationalization is so foolish that it actually makes one laugh as shown below.

If we are to believe the above rationalization, then that means that God can change his laws or judicial decisions regarding any issue, in this specific case, the issue of sexual behavior, depending upon whatever reason God deems fit at that moment. So, if we follow this line of logic, let us see where we end up.

So, this means, that if tomorrow, we found ourselves in a situation where the God of the Bible might see fit to bring incest back, and makes incest legal again; how many Christians are going to follow this directive? If tomorrow, the world were to end due to some man-made (such as nuclear war), or alternatively, some Biblical apocalypse, such as a Noah style flood; and God appeared to the one family that he had saved, and commanded them, and said, "go forth, reproduce and populate the earth."

Does that mean that these Christians will now all of a sudden change centuries of prohibition against incest and start having sex with their parents, brothers, and sisters? That is exactly the level of absurdity that the above rationalization entails. It means that there are no fixed laws, or moral values. It means that, when and if God decides again in favor of incest, or commands his followers to have incest, that people will just jump and follow this command?

That is so ludicrous that it shows you just how ludicrous the above rationalization itself is. This all sounds more like what Satan would do, if one existed; not what a wise, benevolent, omnipotent God would do. For more on this, see **CHAPTER C2: SATAN V/S GOD**

Chapter B5: Slavery

FACT: The modern United States does not condone slavery, which directly contradicts the Bible

The Bible approves of and sanctions slavery in multiple places, both in the Old Testament, and the New Testament. There is not much left to the imagination. There are instructions and laws in the Bible as relates to many different kinds of slavery. Note that women get extra special attention in terms of being slaves. Let us examine just some of the many specific teachings of the Bible as relates to slavery, starting with the Old Testament first, and then moving on to the New Testament:

SLAVERY IN THE OLD TESTAMENT:

(1) First and Second level (women) slaves: <u>Exodus 21-21:4</u>

"These are the laws you are to set before them: "if you buy a Hebrew servant, he is to serve you for six years. But in the seventh year, he shall go free, without paying anything. If he comes alone, he is to go free alone; but if he has a wife when he comes, she is to go with him.

If his master gives him a wife and she bears him sons or daughters, the woman and her children shall belong to her master, and only the man shall go free."

There are two different sets of slavery instructions here. The first set relates to the relationship between the master and his slave. The second set is between the master and the wife of the slave, and she has even less rights than the slave.

So, essentially his (the slave's) wife is a second-level slave who may not have the right to leave with her husband, but remains the master's slave even when her husband is set free depending on the situation.

(2) *Selling your daughter as a slave:* <u>*Exodus 21:7-8:*</u>

<u>The Bible next delves into teaching how a man should sell his daughter as a slave:</u>

"If a man sells his daughter as a servant, she is not to go free as male servants do. If she does not please the master who has selected her for himself, he must let her be redeemed. He has no right to sell her to foreigners, because he has broken faith with her.

<u>Note that there are no specific verses on selling your son as a slave, continuing the gender discrimination that is prevalent in the Bible. Presumably, only daughters can be sold as slaves, not sons.</u>

(3) How much to assault a slave:

Exodus 21:20:

The Bible preaches how much to physically assault a slave:

"Anyone who beats their male or female slave with a rod must be punished if the slave dies as a direct result, but they are not be punished if the slave recovers after a day or two, since the slave is their property.

In other words, it is OK to beat a slave to within an inch of his life as long as he recovers in a couple of days.

Exodus 21:26-27:

"An owner who hits a male or female slave in the eye and destroys it must let the slave go free to compensate for the eye. And an owner who knocks out the tooth of a male or female slave must let the slave go free to compensate for the tooth.

In other words, the only punishment a slave owner will suffer for grievously injuring a slave's eye or tooth is that owner will have to set the slave free. There is no other compensation required to be made to the slave, and there is no other civil, or criminal punishment the master will suffer.

ANALYSIS: It should be fairly evident that this is a very primitive, Bronze Age way of thinking and cannot be the word of God unless such a God is a primitive, bronze age God that has no place in modern society. The more reasonable explanation of course is that the Bible is not the word of God, but the word of insufferable, uneducated, Bronze Age peasants.

(4) It is further made clear in the Bible that the Biblical God expects humans to be his slaves as clearly evidenced in Leviticus 25:55:

"For the Israelites belong to me as servants. They are my servants, whom I brought out of Egypt. I am the LORD your God."

Other Biblical translations clearly use the word "slaves" in place of "servants" in the above passages.

(5) It is clear that the Biblical God also expects humans to have slaves and pass them on as possessions as clearly evidenced in Leviticus 25:44-46:

Your male and female slaves are to come from the nations around you; from them you may buy slaves. You may also buy some of the temporary residents living among you and members of their clans born in your country and they will become your property.

You can bequeath them to your children as inherited property and can make them slaves for life, but you must not rule over your fellow Israelites ruthlessly.

(6) Sexual slavery is commanded by the Biblical God in Genesis 16-16:10

Sarai, Abram's wife gives Abram her Egyptian female slave Hagar to take as his wife to produce children; then humiliates her and Hagar runs away. The Biblical God's angels tell Hagar to *"Go back to your mistress and submit to her."*

(7) Sexual slavery of female virgin children per Moses in Numbers 31:14-18

Moses was angry with the officers of the army who returned from the battle. "Have you allowed all the women to live?" he asked them ..... "Now kill all the boys. And kill every woman who has slept with a man, <u>but save for yourselves every girl who has never slept with a man</u>.

<u>In other versions of the Bible, it is clearer that Moses tells his army to preserve for themselves the "*little ones*" among the females who have not slept with a man. Essentially, the God of the Bible is protecting Moses, who is behaving like one big child sexual predator. Is it any wonder that hundreds of Catholic priests sexually abused little children, and were protected by the highest levels of the Vatican?</u>

There are numerous other instances and examples of slavery in the Bible replete with detailed stories.

SLAVERY IN THE NEW TESTAMENT:

Ephesians 6:5:

Slaves, obey your earthly masters with respect and fear, and with sincerity of heart, just as you would obey Christ.

The New Testament itself discusses how to treat and beat slaves; Who should be beaten more and who should be beaten less:

Luke 12:45-48:

But suppose the servant (slave in other Bible versions) says to himself, 'my master is taking a long time in coming,' and he then begins to beat the other servants, both men and women, and to eat and drink and get drunk.

The master of that servant (slave in other Bible versions) will come on a day when he does not expect him and at an hour he is not aware of. He will cut him to pieces and assign him a place with the unbelievers.

The servant (slave in other Bible versions) who knows the master's will and does not get ready or does not do what the master wants will be beaten with many blows. But the one that does not know and does things deserving punishment will be beaten with few blows.

FINAL ANALYSIS AND CONCLUSION:

Essentially, any of the above is abhorrent by today's standards. Slavery is considered unethical, immoral, and illegal in most countries of the world today.

These "teachings" don't have any place in modern society as most developed nations including the United States are against any form of slavery, both literally and metaphorically. This chapter again shows that Biblical guidelines have fallen by the wayside in the trash heap of history where they belong.

Chapter B6: Gender And Age Discrimination

FACT: The modern United States does not allow gender and age discrimination unlike the Bible.

The following are the passages that support and decree in favor of gender and age discrimination in the Bible. Passages from both the Old Testament and the New Testament are represented below:

Leviticus 27-27:7

The LORD said to Moses, "Speak to the Israelites and say to them: 'if anyone makes a special vow to dedicate a person to the LORD by giving the equivalent value, set the value of a male between the ages of 20 years old up to 60 years old at 50 shekels of silver, according to the sanctuary shekel;

For a female, set her value at 30 shekels; for a person from 5 years old up to 20 years old, set the value of the male at 20 shekels and of a female at 10 shekels;

For a person between one month old to 5 years old, set the value of a male at 5 shekels of silver and that of a female at 3 shekels of silver;

For a person 60 years old or more, set the value of a male at 15 shekels and of a female at 10 shekels.

ANALYSIS:

The above passages are crystal clear. The God of the Bible is putting a value on males and females of different ages according to their gender and age. In other words, if we were to tabulate the estimated value of humans based on gender and age in descending order according to the God of the Bible, this is how it would show up:

Male 20-60 years old: 50 shekels
Female 20-60 years old: 30 shekels
Male 5-20 years old: 20 shekels
Male 60 years upward: 15 shekels
Female 5-20 years old: 10 shekels
Female 60 years upward: 10 shekels
Male 1 month - 5 years old: 5 shekels
Female 1 month - 5 years old: 3 shekels

Note that females have less value across the spectrum, adjusted for age; while the younger and elderly have lesser value than adults age 20 to 60 years old. If you notice carefully, in general, females appear to have only 50 to 60% of the value of the equivalent aged male.

<u>**The next time you see any politician or religious leader make the claim that the United States is a Judeo-Christian country, you can present the above chart, and the following New Testament passages to that person:**</u>

<u>**The Status of women in the New Testament does not get much better:**</u>

<u>*1Timothy 2:11-14*</u>:

A woman should learn in quietness and full submission. I do not permit a woman to teach or to assume authority over a man; she must be quiet. For Adam was formed first, then Eve. And Adam was not the one deceived; it was the woman who was deceived and became a sinner.

<u>**The above passages are very clear. Women are to be treated like second class citizens who are not permitted to teach, or be in positions of authority over men. Furthermore, these passages are from the New Testament. Christians cannot write them off as belonging to that pesky Old Testament.**</u>

Furthermore, the above passages mean that it is an act of sacrilege for Biblical Christians to tolerate having women as teachers, mayors, legislators, senators, judges, CEO's, managers, or just about any and all positions where they might have power or authority over a man. The gender discrimination in the Bible is clear. Eve is the one who was deceived, and is the sinner. The implications are clear. Adam was smarter. He is without blame. The woman is

to blame. The man was formed first, so he has a higher position and authority. The woman cannot have a higher position than the man.

Note also that Eve is referred to as "the woman" in the last sentence. Apparently, she is not respectable enough to even have her name said out twice; while Adam's name is used twice. Also, the way the sentence is worded, it is clear that "the woman" is a generalization applicable across the board to all women.

This gender discrimination is further borne out by the subtle way in which women are to blame for other abhorrent things that happen in the Bible as noted below. We return to the Old Testament for this part:

<u>**More on the status of women in the Old Testament:**</u>

Women are to blame for having sex with their father-in-law to raping their own father:

Genesis 38:15-19: Judah is given a free pass to have sexual relations with his daughter-in-law Tamar because he does not recognize her. Tamar is apparently to blame because she has her face covered and does not inform Judah about who she is.

Genesis 19:31-38: Lot's daughters rape him (get him drunk, and have sex with him when he is passed out to get impregnated by him). Again, the man is not guilty because in each case *"he was not aware of it when she lay down or when* *she got up,"* a reference to him being unconscious; essentially making this a two daughters rape their father situation:

One day the older daughter said to the younger, "Our father is old, and there is no man here to give us children - as is the custom all over the earth. Let's get our father to drink wine and then sleep with him and preserve our family line through our father."

That night they got their father to drink wine, and the older daughter went in and slept with him. He was not aware of it when she lay down or when she got up.

The next day the older daughter said to the younger, "Last night I slept with my father. Let's get him to drink wine again tonight, and you go in and sleep with him so we can preserve our family line through our father."

So they got their father to drink wine that night also, and the younger daughter went in and slept with him. Again, he was not aware of it when she lay down or when she got up.

So both of Lot's daughters became pregnant by their father. The older daughter had a son and she named him Moab. The younger also had a son and she named him Ben-Ammi.

So, if the Bible is to be believed, both of Lot's daughters have sex with him while he is passed out (the legal definition of rape today), and produce children. This makes Lot both the father and grandfather to both Moab and Benammi.

If you were to hear a tale like this today, you would be fairly reasonable in thinking that the writer was a deranged, drunk pervert. This is the kind of tale a group of sordidly drunk, perverted, or demented old timers with lustful tendencies towards their own daughters would make sitting around an ancient fire.

However, it is a measure of the extreme backwardness of even modern humans that this tale has apparently been passed off for 2000 years in the Bible, and still believed by many modern humans to be the word of a God. Even if you do believe in the existence of the God of the Bible, and Satan, a reasonable person would be more likely to believe that these words are the work of Satan, and not God.

In fact, if you are a believer, you have to seriously consider as to what would be more representative of Satan if not for him to pass off his words as the words of God to confuse and control mankind. As we look around the world today, isn't it obvious that Satan appears to be in more control all over the world rather than some benevolent, all-knowing and all-powerful God. If one actually believed in the existence of the God of the Bible and of Satan, that would be a more reasonable conclusion.

RATIONALIZATIONS: It is a measure of how deluded some modern religious people are that a so-called Christian woman contacted me about the above references to Lot's daughters having sex with their father, and Tamar having sex with her father-in-law Judah. This woman claimed that Lot's daughters, and Tamar were doing the honorable thing by providing children to their families.

Let us review just how nonsensical this RATIONALIZATION is:

Firstly, if providing children to their families was so honorable, why the necessity for Tamar to dupe Judah by not showing her face before having sex with him, or for Lot's daughters to make their father unconscious with wine (legal definition of rape today), before having sex with him.

These deceitful activities prior to sex make it abundantly clear that there was nothing honorable about it. If this was so honorable, why couldn't Lot have been awake to have sex with his daughters, or Judah to know about the true identity of Tamar. The problem with religion is that it makes even modern humans so insane, that they can come up with outlandish explanations, to keep on believing in a book filled with disgusting stories, just because they were indoctrinated with that book, or those stories as children, and never developed enough critical thinking skills to come out of those delusions.

An unbiased, modern reader, reading these stories for the first time would be entirely within reasonable bounds to conclude that a group of perverted, drunken, likely sexually-starved, primitive men, sat around the fire writing about their deluded, incest-filled fantasies about their own daughters, and daughter-in-laws. It would be a testament to the stupidity of modern humans if they were

to read these stories, and try to come up with justifications or rationalizations as to why they belong in a "holy" book.

<u>Secondly</u>, to go back to the above rationalization, why couldn't an all-powerful, all-knowing God just provide, or create other men for these honorable girls so they would not have to have sex with their father or father-in-law? In fact, let's go all the way back to Genesis. <u>Why was God who created such a vast universe with billions of galaxies, each with billions of stars: not able to create a hundred, or a thousand couples right in the beginning, instead of just Adam and Eve. This solves the **problem of incest** which plagues the Bible currently, as outlined in many previous chapters, to some extent, and provides a large gene pool of population to begin with.</u>

STATUS OF WOMEN AND CHILDREN IN THE MODERN UNITED STATES:

Civil Rights Act of 1964:

The Civil Rights Act of 1964 outlaws discrimination based on race, color, religion, gender or national origin. It is a landmark civil rights and labor law that was enacted by the 88th United States Congress and became effective July 2, 1964 upon being signed into law by President Lyndon Baines Johnson, the 36th President of the United States.

The legislation had been proposed by President John F. Kennedy, the 35th President of the United States, in June 1963, but opposed by filibuster in the Senate at that time.

The assassination of Pres. Kennedy on November 22, 1963 enabled his successor President Johnson to make use of his experience in legislative politics and honor President Kennedy's memory by pushing for the passage of the civil rights bill.

FINAL ANALYSIS AND CONCLUSION:

It is fairly evident from the above, that the Bible is extremely discriminatory towards women and children, and goes so far as to clearly state that the God of the Bible gives different values to men, women and children as tabulated above. In modern Western culture, including the United States of America, there are rules and laws outlawing discrimination on this basis.

Once again, we see that the Bible is on the wrong side of history as far as its views and laws related to gender and age discrimination; and the status of women. Most people calling themselves Christians today subscribe to the more modern view that men and women are equal, and not to the Biblical view that women are inherently of less value than men. This keeps on adding to our evidence that Biblical Christianity just does not exist anymore in the minds of modern Christians.

Chapter B7: Rights
Of The Disabled

F **ACT: The modern United States gives disabled people special privileges, and does not discriminate against them in direct contradiction to the Biblical God:**

The God of the Bible makes it very clear that people with disabilities are not welcome near him; nor are they to approach him with any offerings.

Leviticus 21:16-21

The LORD said to Moses, "Say to Aaron: <u>*'For the generations to come none of your descendants who has a defect may come near to offer the food of his God.*</u>

No man who has any defect may come near: no man who is <u>*blind*</u> *or* <u>*lame,*</u> *disfigured or deformed; no man with a* <u>*crippled foot or hand,*</u> *or who is a* <u>*hunchback*</u> *or a* <u>*dwarf,*</u> *or who has any* <u>*eye defect,*</u> *or who has festering or running sores or damaged testicles.*

No descendant of Aaron the priest who has any defect is to come near to present the food offerings to the LORD. He has a defect; he must not come near to offer the food of his God.

ANALYSIS:

The meaning of the above verses is crystal clear. If you happen to be blind, or lame, or you have had the misfortune of having your hand or foot fractured, or you have any other "defect," you are not welcome in the presence of the God of the Bible; nor are you welcome to present any offerings to him.

It is interesting to wonder why an all-powerful God would be afraid of disabled people coming near him. One would expect an all-powerful, benevolent God to actually do the opposite, and seek out the disabled for the purpose of curing them.

There were no churches back in those days like they exist today. It is clear however, that people who were unfortunate enough to be disabled would not be welcome in church. This goes against our moral and ethical values as a modern society and surely these days disabled people are welcome everywhere. In fact, laws exist to accommodate and help disabled people in every aspect of our society: whether in employment, or jobs, parking facilities, and so on.

However, it is crystal clear that this is not what is taught in the Bible. This is another indication that the Bible is not the word of God, but of intolerant, primitive, ignorant folks with a discriminatory distaste towards the disabled.

STATUS OF THE DISABLED IN THE MODERN UNITED STATES:

Americans with Disabilities Act 1990:

The Americans with Disabilities Act of 1990 is a civil rights law that prohibits discrimination based on disability. It requires covered employers to provide reasonable accommodations to people with disabilities, and imposes accessibility requirements on public accommodations.

It was enacted by the 101st United States Congress and became effective on July 26, 1990 when it was signed into law by President George Herbert Walker Bush, the 41st President of the United States. An amended version was signed into law by his son President George W. Bush, the 43rd President of the United States, with changes effective January 1, 2009.

This ADA Amendments Act of 2008 was enacted by the 110th United States Congress. The amended act clarified and broadened the definition of the term disability, and therefore increased the number and types of persons who are protected under it.

The need for this amendment arose because of the way that the Supreme Court and lower courts were interpreting the original act of 1990. These interpretations were preventing individuals with impairments such as amputation, epilepsy, diabetes, multiple sclerosis, and even cancer from qualifying for protection under the original Americans with Disabilities Act.

In 2004, an independent federal agency called the National Council on Disability, was charged with reporting and making recommendations to the President and the Congress regarding the original ADA. This report "Righting the ADA" showed the various ways that the courts had misinterpreted the intent of the ADA and limited its reach.

From these actions of the federal agency, the President, and the Congress, we can see that every branch of the United States government has worked to establish clear and comprehensive prohibition of discrimination on the basis of disability, and worked to continue to broaden its impact. This, of course, directly contradicts the God of the Bible who actively discriminates against the disabled as we have seen above in the Biblical passages from ***Leviticus 26:16-21.***

FINAL ANALYSIS AND CONCLUSION:

As we have seen numerous times before, the Bible continues to be on the wrong side of history; in this case, on the issue of treatment of the disabled as well. On the one hand, the God of the Bible gives explicit instructions to Moses not to allow any disabled people to come near him. On the other hand, modern Western culture affords disabled people all the protections it can under the law.

Most modern Christians probably do not subscribe to the Biblical view above, but to the more modern accommodative laws of the current United States. Therefore, we keep on seeing that Biblical laws and regulations play less and less of a role in the mind of modern Christians.

Chapter B8: Giving Money To The Poor

FACT: In these modern United States, we don't give away all our money to the poor as the Bible commands

Matthew 19:23-24

Then Jesus said to his disciples "truly I say to you, it is hard for someone who is rich to enter the kingdom of heaven. Again I tell you, it is easier for a camel to go through the eye of a needle than for someone who is rich to enter the kingdom of God."

Luke 18:25:

Indeed, it is easier for a camel to go through the eye of a needle than for someone who is rich to enter the kingdom of God."

Essentially what this means is, if you believe in the God of the Bible, and you are a rich person, you are not going to heaven anyway. There is a zero chance of that happening, since it is fairly evident that there is a zero chance of a camel going through the eye of a needle.

Matthew 6:24-25:

"No one can serve two masters. Either you will hate the one and love the other, or you will be devoted to the one and despise the other. <u>You cannot serve both God and money</u>."

"Therefore I tell you, <u>do not worry about your life, what you will eat or drink; or about your body, what you will wear</u>. Is not life more than food, and the body more than clothes?

Luke 16:13 is similar to Matthew above

"No one can serve two masters. Either you will hate the one and love the other, or you will be devoted to the one and despise the other. <u>You cannot serve both God and money</u>."

How rich or poor do you have to be? That is fairly evident from the Bible as well.

Jesus teaches a rich man who has kept all the other commandments in **Luke 18:22-23:**

When Jesus heard this, he said to him, "<u>You still lack one thing. Sell everything you have and give to the poor, and you will have treasure in heaven.</u> Then come, follow me."

When he heard this, he became very sad, because he was very wealthy.

<u>Essentially, Jesus is saying that even if a person keeps all the commandments, he or she will still not enter the kingdom</u>

of heaven as long as he or she is a rich person. He further clarifies and leaves no doubt that it is impossible for a rich man to enter the kingdom of heaven in both **_Matthew 19:23_** and **_Luke 18:25_** above.

Jesus further says in the Bible regarding riches:

Matthew 6:19-21

Do not store up for yourselves treasures on earth, where moths and vermin destroy, and where thieves break in and steal. But store up for yourselves treasures in heaven, where moths and vermin do not destroy, and where thieves do not break in and steal. For where your treasure is, there your heart will be also._

FINAL ANALYSIS AND CONCLUSION:

The above values that are espoused in the Bible are in direct and complete opposition to as well as being totally inconsistent with the values in all major Western and developed countries including the United States of America. Firstly, we do store up treasures upon this earth in direct contradiction to the Bible. These are in the form of belongings like newer and more expensive cars, houses, furniture, high definition televisions, gold, jewelry, coins, and other collectibles.

We also store up treasures in the form of bank accounts, stocks, bonds, retirement accounts, 401 k plans, real estate, and many other things. We are a consumer driven society. We get the latest clothes, shoes, fashion items, watches, jewelry; dress ourselves up and go sit in church with our Bibles, all the while directly disobeying the laws espoused in the Bible itself as in the above passages. Does this reflect ignorance of the word of the Bible, or defiance of the word of the Bible, or just plain old hypocrisy?

The United States is a capitalist country. We do not hold the pursuit of money and happiness to be a bad thing. In the Bible, a rich man cannot go to heaven. However, in the United States, people are free to assert themselves in accumulating as much wealth as they can. They do not, as the Bible adjudicates them to, give away all their money or possessions to the poor. Yet they claim to be Christians, which according to the above Bible passages, they are most certainly not.

In an interesting perversion of the Bible, some "Christian" televangelists go so far as to ask gullible people to send them money, so they can buy bigger and more luxurious personal items; including, but not limited to, multiple jets for personal travel. Many such incidents have been documented in news articles and other media.

Chapter B9: Tolerating Other Religions

FACT: The United States allows the practice of
different religions in the country including the
practice of having no religion in direct contradiction to
the commands of the God of the Bible.

Exodus 32:7-10

*The LORD said to Moses: "Go down, because your people, whom
you brought up out of Egypt, have become corrupt. They have
been quick to turn away from what I commanded them and have
made an **idol** cast in the shape of a calf.*

*They have bowed down to it and sacrificed to it and have said,
'These are your Gods, Israel, who brought you up out of Egypt.'"*

*"I have seen these people," the LORD said to Moses, "and they
are a stiff necked people. Now leave me alone so that my anger
may burn against them and that I may destroy them, Then I will
make you into a great nation."*

Deuteronomy 12:3

*Break down their altars, smash their sacred stones and burn their Asherah poles in the fire; cut down the **idols** of their gods, and wipe out their names from those places.*

Deuteronomy 32:21

*They made me jealous by what is no god and angered me with their worthless **idols**....*

FINAL ANALYSIS AND CONCLUSION:

In the Bible, it is made very clear in many references that there is no room for believing in other Gods, or their idols, altars, statues, or images, and doing so is punishable by death. Now we all know that many people proclaim that America is a Christian country. However, let us look at the facts. The United States allows the unrestricted practice of all religions or no religion. It is built on a secular foundation, with separation of church and state.

Even prayers of different religions (such as Hindu prayers) have occurred in the U.S. Senate, U.S. Congress, and other government buildings. Note that ***Exodus 32:8*** and ***Deuteronomy 12:3*** specifically forbid idol worship which is a specific hallmark of Hinduism. In Hinduism, the cow is also considered sacred which again directly contradicts the God of the Bible in *Exodus 32:8*.

Deuteronomy 32:21 comes out even more clearly against idol worship. So, if you grant the idea that there is a God as detailed in the Bible, the very action of tolerating, or bringing in a preacher of a different God, or Gods is heretical in nature; and against the teachings of the God of the Bible. **The United States, therefore, cannot be considered a Christian country according to the above Biblical verses.**

Chapter B10: Turning The Other Cheek

F ACT: The United States does not turn the other cheek when it's enemies attack it.

Matthew 5:38-41

"You have heard that it was said, 'Eye for eye and tooth for tooth.' But I tell you, do not resist an evil person. If anyone slaps you on the right cheek, turn to them the other cheek also. And if anyone wants to sue and take your shirt, hand over your coat as well. If anyone forces you to go one mile, go with them two miles.

Luke 6:27-30 essentially has Jesus saying the same thing:

"But to you who are listening I say: Love your enemies, do good to those who hate you, bless those who curse you, pray for those who mistreat you. If someone slaps you on one cheek, turn to them the other also. If someone takes your coat, do not withhold your shirt from them. Give to everyone who asks you, and if anyone takes what belongs to you, do not demand it back."

ANALYSIS:

Note that Matthew and Luke are a little inconsistent with each other as to which garment comes off first. Luke has the outer garment coming off first, and Matthew has the inner garment coming off first. **However, the message in the above passages is crystal clear. Essentially, Jesus is saying that if somebody takes one of your garments, you should give up your other garment also to that person.**

Similarly, if somebody slaps you on one of your cheeks, you should offer them your other cheek as well. Jesus also says you should not resist a wicked person, but should continue to love your enemies, and do good to them. The essential concept above is that if anybody asks something from you, you should give it up, and not ask for it back.

These particular set of principles are actually very admirable. However, we don't follow them in our modern culture. We have teams of lawyers that fight for us as individuals and as corporate organizations. We have a very antagonistic legal system and set of rules; as far as our modern culture goes, and none more so than in the United States.

Whether it is a neighborly dispute, whether it is a divorce, whether it is a corporate battle or take over, whether it is state's rights versus federal rights, we have a well-developed court and judicial system to fight for every inch of our rights; whether they be property rights, intellectual rights, or other rights too numerous to list here.

Our whole modern system in these United States is completely antithetical and goes completely against the aforementioned particular teachings in the Bible, showing once more that we are not, and cannot be considered a Christian country.

Similarly, we don't turn the other cheek when confronted with potentially cruel or evil circumstances. We did not let Hitler continue to invade and take countries to his liking. The allies stepped up and fought back, and defeated the "Axis of evil." The allies including the U.S., Britain, and others stood up to Hitler when he wanted to invade more and more countries. They did not give him more than what he wanted.

Other examples include Iraq and Afghanistan. <u>In fact, U.S. presidents like George W. Bush went one step further and even did preemptive wars, all the while calling themselves Christians, in direct contradiction of the New Testament and Jesus' teachings above.</u> Thus, Jesus' teachings sound very naïve and misplaced in the modern world, and nobody, least of all United States Presidents' appear to follow them. As if the aforementioned passages in the Bible were not clear enough, here is more from Jesus:

<u>*Matthew 5:43-48*</u>

You have heard that it was said, 'Love your neighbor and hate your enemy.' But I tell you, <u>love your enemies and pray for those who persecute you, that you may be children of your Father in heaven.</u>

He causes his sun to rise on the evil and the good, and sends rain on the righteous people and the unrighteous. If you love those who love you, what reward will you get? Are not even the tax collectors doing that? *And if you greet only your own people, what are you doing more than others? Do not even pagans do that? Be perfect, therefore. as your heavenly Father is perfect.*

Matthew 6:14-15

For if you forgive other people when they sin against you, your heavenly Father will also forgive you. But if you do not forgive others their sins, your Father will not forgive your sins.

FINAL ANALYSIS AND CONCLUSION:

All of the passages in this chapter illustrate that Jesus wanted all Christians to love their enemies; not just their neighbors, or families. However, in the United States, this does not happen. We continue to hate or demonize presumptive "enemies" like Russia, Iraq, Afghanistan, or North Korea. The Democrats and Republicans continue to battle and hate each other 24 hours a day, seven days a week, in any and all form of media, including, but not limited to MSNBC, FOX, or as evidenced by jokes in late night comedy shows, like Stephen Colbert, Seth Meyers, and so on. Therefore, we don't really behave like a Christian country, or a Christian people, per The New Testament.

Section C: Conclusion

Chapter C1: Direct Links Between The Old And New Testament

Some so-called Christians that I talk to tend to rationalize all the incest, polygamy, sexual slavery, gender and age discrimination, and other terrible things in the Old Testament by saying that they don't really read or believe in the Old Testament. In other words, they tend to ignore it, and tend to focus more on the New Testament.

However, there is inherently no logic to this. It is made very clear in multiple places in the Bible that the New Testament is the continuation of the Old Testament, and that Jesus is the son of the God mentioned in the Old Testament. He does not claim to be the son of a different God from a different religion, or religious book, nor does he claim to be a new God completely superseding the God of the Old Testament. He is drawing his power squarely from the God of the Old Testament. So we cannot just ignore or throw away the Old Testament with regards to Jesus.

<u>Jesus himself clarifies many times that he is the son of the
God of the Old Testament:</u>

John 5:18-19

*For this reason they tried all the more to kill him; not only was he
breaking the Sabbath, but <u>he was also calling God his own father,
making himself equal with God. Jesus gave them this answer:
"Very truly I tell you, the Son can do nothing by himself; he can
do only what he sees his Father doing."</u>...*

John 5:30

*"By myself I can do nothing; I judge only as I hear, and my
judgment is just, for I seek not to please myself but him who
sent me."*

<u>The direct line from the Old Testament to the New Testament
can be found in numerous other places in the Bible as well.</u>

Per Matthew 1:3 Judah of the Old Testament became father
to Perez and Zerah by Tamar. Thereafter, Perez became
father to Hezron.

Matthew 1:3 to 1:16 traces the direct lineage from Judah to
Perez to Hezron and various other intermediaries to *"Joseph
the husband of Mary of whom Jesus was born who is called
Christ."*

Thus Joseph is the descendant of the son Perez of Judah and his daughter-in-law Tamar (referred to as a harlot) in _**Genesis 38:24.**_ This episode has been detailed elsewhere in this book.

That Jesus is the son of the God of the Old Testament is also intimated in _**Matthew 3:17:**_

And a voice from heaven said, "This is my Son, whom I love; with him I am well pleased."

Furthermore, Jesus goes on to indicate in Luke 12:51-53 that he did not come to give peace on earth. He makes it fairly clear that he is here to sow division:

Luke 12:51-53:

"Do you think I came to bring peace on earth? No, I tell you, but division. From now on there will be five in one family divided against each other, three against two and two against three. They will be divided, father against son and son against father, mother against daughter and daughter against mother, mother-in-law against daughter-in-law and daughter-in-law against her mother-in-law."

Furthermore, Jesus makes it pretty clear that not a letter of the law of the Old Testament can be ignored in _**Matthew 5:17-19:**_

"Do not think that I have come to abolish the law or the Prophets. I have not come to abolish them but to fulfill them. For truly I tell you, until heaven and earth disappear, not the smallest letter, *not the least stroke of a pen, will by any means disappear from the law until everything is accomplished.* Therefore anyone who sets aside one of the least of these Commands and teaches others accordingly will be called least in the kingdom of heaven.

FINAL ANALYSIS AND CONCLUSION:

It is fairly obvious from the passages above that all of the incest, polygamy, sexual slavery, gender and age discrimination, and other terrible things in the Old Testament (plus The New Testament), cannot just be ignored or thrown away by modern Christians in their quest to sanitize the Bible. Jesus himself claims power directly from the God of the Old Testament, and commands that every letter of the law of the Old Testament is valid.

Chapter C2: Satan v/s God

In the Bible, it is made very clear that the God of the Bible is the sole and only decision maker, or mover and shaker that there is. There is no division of labor with God doing all the good things, and the other fictional character, Satan, doing all the bad things. God does it all by himself as in the following verses:

Isaiah 45:6-7:

"..... I am the LORD, and there is no other. I form the light and create darkness, I bring prosperity and create disaster; I, the LORD, do all these things."

I want everyone to be able to consider the following very carefully: When you think of somebody with possibly unlimited power, who is self-obsessed about being worshiped; extols the killing of children, the rape of women, and gives blessing to sleeping with your own daughters and siblings, slavery, and so forth, who comes to mind?

If you truly believe in the existence of both God and Satan, then the answer is crystal clear. Satan is who comes to mind, not God. What else do we know about Satan? Again, if you believe in the whole Satan and God story, we know that Satan is very cunning, and uses all manners of trickery and delusion to fool people and gain control of their mind.

Once you begin following the logic above, then isn't it possible, that Satan discovered that the biggest illusion of all to gain control and power over people would be to fool them into thinking that he was God? Isn't it possible then, that the entire work of the Bible is not God's word, but the work of Satan passing himself off as God?

This is a mind blowing revelation, but it makes perfect sense. Is not the God of our imagination much different than the God of the Bible, as we have uncovered in this book? Would the God of our imagination condone killing children, raping women, sleeping with our daughters and siblings, condone slavery, and all other manner of debauchery which is exactly what the Biblical God does.

It is as if Satan is having fun with us, if he exists at all. These passages are not even subtle, or hidden; on the contrary, they are clearly out in the open, for anyone to read. And yet in 2000 years, not enough people have picked up on these passages to initiate a widespread and serious discussion about how the God of the Bible does not measure up to the God of our imagination, but resembles that other fictional entity: Satan.

What then, if by some ironic twist of fate, the so-called atheists are unknowingly themselves the real

messengers of God, by bringing attention to the problem characteristics of the pretend God of the Bible. Maybe the real God is indeed waiting out there for another Messiah to uncover the ugly truth about Satan; that is, if you believe in that sort of thing. It would follow then, that in this alternate scenario, these so-called atheists are themselves unknowingly the true people of God, who unbeknownst to them are uncovering the illusion that Satan has created, thereby doing God's work.

Isn't it time to consider who benefits most from the teachings of the Bible? Is it God? Or is it Satan? Are believers in the Bible going to hell or nonbelievers? I think once you have read the Bible, the answer is crystal clear. The following people have no chance of entering the kingdom of heaven, as we have seen from previous chapters:

(1) rich people (according to the Bible, this includes anyone who has not given away all of their money to the poor, as has been shown in a previous chapter of this book)

(2) adulterers (adulterers, according to the Bible include divorced people who remarry, as has been shown in an earlier chapter of this book)

(3) homosexuals

(4) disabled

The list goes on. Since this list covers the vast majority of the people in the Western world (there are very few people in the western world who are not rich and / or not divorced), **it stands to follow that almost everyone is actually going to hell. If you believe in the whole God and Satan dynamic, it is easy to see that Satan is the one who benefits, and not God**.

Doesn't it logically follow that the Bible is indeed the word of Satan, as it is he who benefits most from it by sending the vast majority of people to hell? That is indeed, a more reasonable conclusion, if we continue to insist in believing in a fantasy world that has a fantasy God and a fantasy Satan.

Other interesting evidence can be found in numerous Old Testament verses such as the one below in which the God of the Bible commands Moses as follows:

Exodus 30-30:5

*"Make an altar of acacia wood for burning incense. It should be square, a cubit long and a cubit wide, and two cubits high- it's horns of one piece with it. Overlay the top and all the sides and the horns with pure **gold**, and make a **gold** molding around it.*

*Make two **gold** rings for the altar below the molding- two on each of the opposite sides- to hold the poles used to carry it. Make the poles of acacia wood and overlay them with **gold**.*

If we take the New Testament verses discussed in Chapter B8 as fact, **that a rich man cannot enter the kingdom of heaven, then how are we supposed to perceive the Old Testament verses dealing with a God who seems to be**

obsessed with gold? Why would a good and decent God be obsessed with gold, when Jesus himself has intimated to us in many verses (**see Chapter B8**), that having gold and riches is a bad thing, and unworthy of heaven.

There are many other verses in the Bible that show the obsession of the Biblical God with gold. It would follow then that God himself cannot enter the kingdom of heaven, which makes essentially no sense. Isn't it a more logical and reasonable conclusion that the supernatural entity commanding Moses, was actually not God, but Satan; for who would be one that cannot enter the kingdom of heaven, if not Satan?

FINAL ANALYSIS AND CONCLUSION:

By now, at the end of this book, we have read and uncovered all manner of debauchery, evil, and incest attributable to the Biblical God. This is only the tip of the iceberg. The more you read the Bible, the more evidence of all manner of bad things are uncovered. By now, hopefully, the reader has been presented with enough information, facts, logic, and evidence to realize that the Bible is obsolete in the modern world, and that God is just a primitive fantasy.

However, if for some unfathomable reason, the reader is still inclined to believe in a Biblical God, one must still admit that it is not possible to differentiate between the two fictional entities: Satan and God. But don't just take my word for it. Just go ahead and review the verse at the beginning of this Chapter presented again below:

Isaiah 45:6-7:

"..... I am the LORD, and there is no other. I form the light and create darkness, I bring prosperity and create disaster; I, the LORD, do all these things."

There you have it. The Bible says it clearly enough via ***Isaiah 45:6-7:*** **Satan is God. God is Satan. There is only one fictional entity and no other.**

Section D: Index For Biblical Verses

THE END

9 781480 871984